# *Hope Reigns*

*A Journey from Domestic Violence*

Mary Farmer

Copyright 2015 by Mary Farmer
Published 2015.
Printed in the United States of America.

All rights reserved.

No portion of this book may be reproduced, stored in a retrieval system, or transmitted in any form or by any means – electronic, mechanical, photocopy, recording, scanning, or other – except for brief quotations in critical reviews or articles, without the prior written permission of the author.

ISBN 978-1-943659-03-3

Library of Congress Control Number 2015948905

Cover design by Amanda Featherston.

www.amandafeatherston.com

This book was published by BookCrafters,
Parker, Colorado.
bookcrafters@comcast.net
This book may be ordered from
www.bookcrafters.net

and other online bookstores.

## *Acknowledgements*

I spent my entire childhood reading books which fostered the dream of someday writing my own. God saw my heart and I'm grateful that he is a loving Father who tends to the most intimate details of our hearts.

I'm thankful for my daughter, Amanda, and my husband, Kevin, who kept the encouragement coming when I wanted to give up and quit writing. Thank you. I love you both so much.

Another thank you to Amanda Featherston, my beautiful and talented offspring, for the cover design and photography. You are amazingly talented in all that you do.

Thank you to Brenda and Susie for your hard work editing this work. Thankyou Meemaw, AKA Linda, and Shelli for your help as well. You took a diamond in the rough and made it shine. I am blessed to you call you friends.

God bless all of the survivors who have lived my story. I pray you will find healing, courage and hope in the pages of this book.

To all the survivors I have had the privilege of working with as your advocate: I dedicate this book to YOU. I hope this book will help others understand the answer to the question we are always asked: *"Why don't you just leave?"* Leaving is harder than staying. I get it and I hope the world will get it too.

## *Foreword*

It's about abuse … and I couldn't put it down. Mary's book, Hope Reigns. Everything else automatically went to the back burner and I sat reading in suspense … from the very first sentence onward. Hers is more than a novel; its tension and heartache wrapped up in her self-styled personal narrative. And that's what makes it a top ten on my list is that fact. It has the feel of a novel but it is NOT FICTION; it's her own real life's story of tragedy … and victory. It shows how God Himself is working in the affairs of men and circumstances to bring about rescue.

"Why don't you just leave?" is the question too often asked of the abused. You will see here some of the reasons why it's just not that simple. It starts with the sweet joy of tender new love. Then, once the trust is secure, then comes first a fragment of shocking anger, but a quick apology. Then, comes a slap, followed by another apology. Then, it's another and another, with slow degradation. And emotional harm, hidden bruises and a crushed soul. And before you know it, you're in a cesspool of whirling muck-water, trapped by intimidation, or by presence of a child to protect, or by threats toward parents or job, or even the threat against your own life. "Just leave" ... if it were only that simple.

It's not simple. But it IS possible. It takes courage. It takes prayer. There is hope.

Mary's story here shows others who are also abused, both women and men, whether it be in their marriages, their live-in situations, their jobs, whatever their circumstances, there is hope for them. And it doesn't matter how serious, how demeaning, how tragic their lives are, Hope Reigns! Mary illustrates how there are open doors. There is escape. There are walls, yes, but there are open windows and gates with people standing there with welcoming arms. And those people are sent by God to help, whether those servants know it or not.

Mary found them. And if you are a Mary, you can find them too.

Mary lifts Him up; it's God who is the hero in this play, in this real-life drama. It's HIM saving the lives of both Mary and her daughter, Manda.

Mary becomes the "Miss Barnabas" of encouragement for you here in her book. Hope Reigns and you can find it too.

Larry West
Author; Speaker, Director, We Care Ministries

*Part 1: The Escape*

# Chapter 1

## April 19, 2002

As the clock on the dash flashed the time, a sinking feeling began to rise in the pit of my stomach. I sped down the dark country roads toward our house. *Every minute that passed was another offense against me.* Twenty minutes is nothing to some, a miniscule fragment of time, worth nothing in the grander scheme of life, but to me it could be the difference between life and death.

Heart pounding in my chest, I gripped the steering wheel as I navigated around the bumps and ruts in the potted road ahead of me. Minutes continued to tick by as my daughter and I tried to race the incoming storm home with the hopes that he wasn't there yet. We were late. We had missed that narrow window of time that I was allowed to go to church and get back home.

One more turn and we would be almost home. I wanted to believe it was going to be okay. So many times in the past Manda and I would pull into the driveway and be so grateful that the truck was gone. We were safe for a moment, but how long would it last? Somehow even before I saw the headlights and the vehicle careening towards us, I knew. I just knew.

We both saw it at the same time. Manda began to cry in the seat next to me.

"I'm sorry Mom ... I'm sorry! I didn't mean to get you in trouble."

My heart melted at the desperation in her voice. Fourteen years of sadness. Guilt and shame welled up within me and washed over my soul like a heart-wrenching flood. I hated myself for all those times in the night when I would promise God we would leave if I survived but when the sun came up, I stayed. I raged inside my head as I watched him speed toward us for all of the years she had suffered for my decisions. She deserved better. She deserved a mom and a dad who loved her. She deserved a life with parties and dances and friends. Amanda deserved to come home from school each day confident that I was alive and safe instead of the stark dread of not knowing what she would find.

As the truck drew closer with a madman behind the wheel, I braced myself for an impact. Never quite sure what he would do when he got in that state, I was preparing my heart to die.

"It's not your fault, sweetie. It's okay. It's

going be okay…. There is *nothing* wrong with us getting an ice cream."

How stupid the words sounded even to my own ears. What normal person even has to even question such a thing? Why? Why? Why? Was I such a horrible person that I deserved this fate? Was my fate to die and him to live? Had I committed a sin so great that this was my punishment? What had Amanda done to deserve this hell of a life, for that is what it was.

Suddenly the truck was next to us and he slammed on the brakes. In my mirror I saw the truck slide sideways behind me. My foot pressed the brake knowing there was no escape. Not now. It wouldn't do any good to try. Trying would just make it worse. I wasn't sure if I was expected to stop or continue on the final few miles to our house. The answer was quickly apparent as he spun the truck around behind me, veered around me and flew ahead in a scary burst of speed. Anger poured from the truck like a visible cloud, and I half-feared *and* half-hoped that he would crash and settle it all before we reached the house.

Amanda began to cry and I began to search for that place in my mind that didn't feel anything. I had learned to do that over the years. I became an ice princess where nothing could touch my soul. My physical body would cry and beg for my life, but there was a place that even he couldn't reach. He couldn't. It wasn't his. It was mine. Once again, I would play his vicious hateful game of cat and mouse, but if he won? He wouldn't win.

Our trailer beckoned for us to come home as we pulled into the driveway, the home where my grandparents had lived before their death. Home, where Grandpa loved his girl. Memories of a loving place had now become my prison. Slowly, I inched my Buick into the space beside his truck. He already stood waiting in the driveway. Amanda cowered in fear of her daddy, but still, as always, she tried to protect me.

"I'm sorry, Daddy, It's my fault. I'm sorry."

My little girl, who wanted nothing more in this world than for her daddy to love her, tried to bridge the gap on my behalf. I was both scared for her and proud of her courage. At times she refused to back down and it usually cost us both. I wanted so badly for her to be his little princess. Her brown eyes matched his with expressions that said they could be twins. His DNA proudly coursing through her veins. Brown eyes met a mirror reflection as she implored for mercy on my behalf, but his heart was set like a stone. This person we both loved and hated, who was both my judge and jury, had already handed down my sentence. Her soul, connected through love and pain to mine, wanted to absorb guilt so that

I could go free. My arms ached to hold her and kiss away her heartache. I prayed that somehow God would fix this awful mess. How did we get here? To this time? To this place? I shivered in the driveway as I knew there was no escaping what was about to happen. Once the lock clicked on the door, it would be a very, very long night.

Totally ignoring the pleas from his only child, he said, "Get your A… in the house."

She knew better than to say it again. It would only make it worse for me. As she walked to her room, I wished she could escape from her prison without locks. She knew the rules. She couldn't come back out. No matter what. All of the endless long nights for my beautiful, precious, perfect little girl to spend crying herself to sleep, needing to go to the bathroom, needing to know her momma was okay, and feeling guilty because there was nothing she could do to save me. The thin walls of our mobile home only served to intensify the noises, so she would raise the volume of the television to block out the cries in the stillness of the night.

Softly, I laid purse and Bible on the dining room table as I tried to search him out in the blackness of his mind. What was the trigger that ignited *this* particular inferno? Was it really the broken curfew? Was it someone at work? Did he get in a fight? Was his back hurting? The source was never relevant because the punishment would always be mine.

The silence in the house was deafening. I could hear the pounding of my heart beating through my chest. To calm the man who could change in an instant I had to stay calm. Much of the world saw a charming man with big brown eyes who would help strangers on the side of the road or snuggle babies on his knee and laugh. That was the man Amanda and I longed for and loved. He was the one that we needed to be our protector. He was also the one we needed to be protected from.

"Who were you talking to? I know you were talking to someone. Was it Stan? I know it was. I was there, you know. I SAW you."

"You didn't see anything. I wasn't talking to anyone. Go ask your mom or any of your family." The old familiar drill rising up again. It was dreadful and repetitive and exhausting. The endless mind games and questioning for hours upon end. My soul became weary and aged in just a moment's time. My soul was tired. So tired. Endless interrogations, over the years, put my nerves on edge every time I had to speak. Constant precautions in place for every aspect of life to prevent a night like this. No matter the lengths I went to trying to avoid ever having to speak to a man, or breaking a rule that I couldn't share, covering up the truth and wearing a mask. It was never enough.

I knew I had done nothing wrong on this night, but that was not the point. To him, I was guilty. I was guilty of not being able to fix what was broken inside him, and my punishment was going to be great. The pain that raged inside of him became unleashed on me. This was my fate. This was my life. I was his wife.

The interrogation went on for a bit and I was surprised as his fury seemed to wind down in a miraculous way I wasn't expecting. Dare I hope that it was over? Please, God, let it be! What a wonderful gift that would be! Would he accept that it was simply an ice cream cone and not something more?

Cautiously, I prepared for bed. A nightgown left me vulnerable to the dark, cold of the night. If I needed to escape, fully clothed was the better option. I knew this from experience. Trying to leave clothes where I could get to them was not always an option, but the thought was always there. Just in case.

Lying in bed, the television projecting voices that I cared not about, I felt the slightest glimmer of hope that it was done. He stretched out on the bed beside me and began to talk about something the newscaster had said. I felt the tension start to go out of my body and I began to relax. As he lay on his back watching the television, I felt safe to turn onto my stomach and settle down for the night. The quiet in the house was deceptive.

I had barely turned over and closed my eyes, when suddenly I felt a shift of his weight as he moved with the grace of an experienced assassin. Suddenly I couldn't breathe as his vice-like hand covered my mouth and nose while his other arm surrounded my neck. I clawed at his arms to release me. I was pinned to the bed by his 200 pound frame half-sitting, half-lying across my back and waist. I couldn't move. Panic rushed over me like a wave. Every moment I couldn't breathe, the terror raged more and more inside of me. Spots began to float in front of my eyes. My head and neck began to go numb. It was the oddest sensation not being able to capture life sustaining air. The seconds seemed endless as they ticked by and he continued to maintain his grip. I prayed desperately and tried to cry out, but he only increased his hold. "OH MY GOD! HE'S GOING TO KILL ME!" Demon vultures of death swirled above me in my mind's eye, mocking me in laughter, taunting me with their truth, my agonizing terror made real!

My baby, my life, my heartbeat was literally only feet away from us across the hall. I wasn't going to be able to tell her how much I loved her or how very sorry I was. So sorry. For everything that was her life. The all too familiar shotgun was only inches from my head. I recounted all of the times in the past where he had held pillows over my face. I compared those endless seconds ticking by—each precious, life giving, tick. Never had he held me this long.

Just when the spots started to come and go in my consciousness and I felt moments of reality slipping away, he suddenly released me only to shift his position and mine. In just a matter of seconds I was flipped onto my back, pinned under his weight. I desperately searched his face looking for that glimmer in his eyes that melted me in a flash. The boyish grin that everyone loved. I prayed he would love me and end this madness before it was too late.

The face I saw was not the face of the man I had married. He was different. Altered. Evil had replaced all of the goodness that I knew was buried within. His soul had surrendered to that other self. I searched desperately to find the man who had once loved me with sweet passion and eyes that had looked at me with boyish devotion. All of the childlike promises mocked me in the hate resonating from his dark, glassy-eyed stare. A darkness settled over him. It was as if there was a shadow of a man behind him, a puppet master, fully in control. The man I married was defenseless against this master manipulator of power and control. That vow of love once between us was replaced with a torrid gut-wrenching pain of betrayal and destruction. Neither one of us could escape this horrible production that was our reality. How it would play out, for both of us, was yet to be seen.

An all too familiar gleam came into his eye and I wasn't surprised to see the white of the pillow covering my face. This pattern, this battle for eternity, was raging within both of our souls. It was a battle of wills, this stealthy ballet of evil verses good, of which there would be no winners. To both of us there was a cost. The stage was this room, this bed, this place, this moment in time. The scene replayed from the beginning of time. This puppet master, seeking total control, slipping in from home to home, setting the stage, whispering words of deception and lies into unwitting ears, hoping to hear applause from the flames of hell as another family is vanquished.

As instinct replaced rational thought, my body began to fight for air as the pillow took the place of his hand and reality once again began to spin out of control. Years of practice proved my expertise as I wiggled and inched toward the edge of the bed. His total focus was on snuffing out any vestige of air, closing off any path of escape, and bringing me under complete subjection to his will. Turning my head just enough, I was able to inhale fresh air before he discovered that precious air had filled my lungs. It was over as it quickly as it had begun. I lay on the bed gasping for air. Warily I watched, preparing for the next attack.

"You're a liar! Why do you always have to lie to me? Skank! You stupid slut!" Round after round of shots to the heart. Each one struck its intended target. The years of staying strong had taken an unexpected toll upon my heart. No longer able to withstand the attack, the pieces of my heart disintegrated and disappeared. Nothing in life seemed to matter anymore. I didn't even really care, in that moment, if I lived or died. Death was preferable to another day of that life! My fear in that moment was that death wouldn't come easy and it wouldn't be kind.

I watched from the edge of the bed as he paced around the room. So many ways to die in that room. Guns, bows, razor sharp broad head arrows, custom hunting knives… all within easy reach. Surely my soul would be saved. Surely I wouldn't truly burn in hell as he had often promised I would. I just prayed it would come easy.

He left the room but quickly returned. Fleeing was pointless. I would never make it out the door. With his back to me, he did something by the dresser. As he moved back to my side, hysteria bubbled forth and I couldn't contain it. I had to fight or my death would be long and painful.

"Put it in your mouth!" I stared in disbelief as he handed me a baggie with a sock inside. He expected me to gag myself. He also held a neck tie. *Oh Dear God, not again. Please, not again. I can't take that again.* I felt the pieces of my sanity quickly slipping away. Memories of other times and other places… other nights with my hands bound as my body took the beating. Unable to move or escape.

"I'm not putting that in my mouth."

"Do it!"

*"NO!" God, please don't let him do it. Please, don't let him.* I hoped that bargaining with God would somehow release me from this nightmare. Something seemed to change inside of him and he tossed the baggie back on the dresser. I was afraid to move. He was like a caged lion, roaming back and forth, issuing insults and forcing me to beg for my life. The inhumanity of begging for the life that belongs to you is a feeling like no other. He came toward me again, this time with a leather belt in hand. I stared at him, eyes wide open, unsure of what was coming next. As I sat on the bed, he stood over me and placed the belt around my neck. He began turning the ends that he held in his hands tighter and tighter until I

realized what he was doing. I clawed and gasped to get it from around my neck.

"I'm going to put you in the truck and take you out into the woods and I'm going to do this until you pass out. I'm going to do it over and over again… and no one will ever know."

A sick sense of dread coupled with adrenalin coursed through my veins. I had been in those woods with him before. The whole incident came flooding back. I could almost feel the cool of the night and hear the sound of the woods at night.

*A few years before, he seemed to drive forever before going down dirt trails back into the protected forest owned by the state. Farther and farther he drove into the woods, all the while hitting me and slamming my head into the windows. Forcing me to strip naked and give him my glasses, he dragged me out of the car into the night air.*

*"This is where people dump dead bodies. They don't find them for years. I'm going to leave you out here... like that… to find your way out of these woods alone." I stood there in my nakedness, full of shame, before the man who had professed he would cherish me always.*

*"Now, run!" My head jerked to attention as I realized he had gotten back into the car and was coming toward me. I ran off the trail and hid behind a tree. He got out of the car and dragged me back to*

*the trail... I stood there... The lights on the car were headed straight for me. I began to run...*

If evil were alive and had a home, it was in those woods. I never wanted to enter that dark place again. I knew without a doubt that he was capable of all that he had spoken. His eyes watched me closely for my response. Quickly, I tried to cover my fear and hide the terror that I felt.

"I'm so sorry. Please, forgive me. Please, don't hurt me!" Perhaps the madman would be appeased by my begging. He released the belt, as if in a trance and tossed it on the bed. "Please, let me leave... if you don't want to be married to me anymore. I'll just go. You can have everything. I promise. Just let me go..." He would never let me go. I knew this already. I wasn't human. I had no rights. I was property. His property.

If only I could convince him of the depth of my love for him. I needed him. For some strange, twisted reason, I wanted him, no—I needed him to know that I loved him. Why couldn't he see it? Was my sacrifice of self not enough? I had given up everything to be his wife. I had nothing left to leave at his altar. I was a shattered remnant of the person I was before. I had given him every ounce of me and yet my gift was not enough. Night continued its journey and the torment continued throughout, hitting, begging, groveling, accusations and fear.

The tirade, mingled with slaps and blows, continued into the early hours of the morning as my strength began to fade away. Nearly at my breaking point, I would have done almost anything to make the nightmare stop. With a calm hand, he picked up the shotgun. My mind had been stretched beyond its limits as weariness of the moment permeated my soul. I no longer cared if I lived or died. I just wanted this night to end. I closed my eyes as I heard him load a slug into the chamber of the gun. I felt cold steel touch my head.

"Pray!" I had never stopped. The room felt cold and stark much like the remnants of my heart. "I'm going to kill you and then I'm going to kill myself."

Hollow, empty words I had heard before. It really mattered not to me what happened anymore, except for Amanda. She was still in her room, alone. She had been there all night. She had to be safe. She had to live. Her precious life was my legacy. The bond between mother and child is like no other. The need to protect and nurture and save, it only grows stronger. It never dims. So many memories of nights spent alone, with a bottle of pills in my hand, as I stared into nothingness trying to find a reason to continue living. She was that reason.

"If you kill me and you kill yourself, you'll

leave Amanda an orphan." I prayed my ploy of diversion would work to distract him from his task. I clung to the thought and hoped that somewhere deep inside him, he desperately loved his daughter. However, I had underestimated the power of the puppet master.

"Don't worry… I'll take care of that."

Inside every person is an imaginary, but very real, line that once it is crossed there is no turning back. As I processed his simple statement, the truth of what he was saying sank to the pit of my soul like hot molten lead. I felt myself slowly, yet deliberately, taking that final step to the point of no return. The last vestige of hope was gone. I would have used the last shred of love that I could muster up to end his misery, if I could have just gotten the gun. Even the value of my life and his really didn't matter in the larger scope of things. That beautiful soul, who loved to draw, and loved princesses and wanted to be a fashion designer, deserved to live. The hellish audience would not get a bow from the master… not on my watch… not if I could help it.

"I'll do anything you want. Just don't hurt Amanda."

Never, not a single time in fourteen years, would I ever have thought it would come to this. That the words could even form in his mouth was almost too much. Bloodline, lineage, family, none of it meant anything. The lies and delusions had stolen something from his heart, something precious, something sweet, something pure: a father's love for his daughter. What a tragedy. How could this be? The beautiful child that had cleaned and done chores to buy him camping equipment for Father's Day so they could go camping together... the artist who had made him cards on notebook paper and spent hours making them perfect, trying to earn the love of the man she needed so much. How had it come to this?

"I hate you!" he hissed. *I know*, my heart cried out.

One more torment. Another threat. Surely the night couldn't last much longer. For some reason, he put the gun back in its place and sat on the edge of the bed. Tears welling in his eyes. The puppet master weaving a web of guilt with his manipulation had us both in his trap of lies. "I don't know why you do these things to me! Why do you have to make me SO MAD? WHY? Tell me why!" As he spoke those words from his twisted place of despair, a final wave of anger ravaged his exhausted body. The night had taken its toll.

In a final fit of rage, he threw me back on the bed, full circle, back to the beginning. I saw the white of the pillow once again. My weary body almost too tired to fight, bucked in one final protest as he knuckled down his grip. Instinctively, I once again tried to get my head to the edge of the bed. This time, he was on to my ploy for air. As he grabbed me to pull me back onto the bed, we both slipped from the bed and landed in a heap on the floor. That's when I heard the snap in my back as his entire weight landed on my torso. The odd angle at which I was laying made it impossible to move and the excruciating pain seared through my entire being. Tears flooded my eyes as I struggled to sit up.

"I can't get up!"

The puppet master released his grip and quickly the little boy expression was back. This time it was an expression of fear. He had gone too far this time. Way too far.

Mercifully, his arms reached down and he lifted me to the bed. I forced myself not to cringe at his touch. I lay there, on the bed, gasping from pain, trying to catch my breath, as a terrifying thought struck me of a life and a future in a wheel chair — at his mercy for a lifetime. Death be merciful and come quickly… I inched myself up on the bed into my spot near the wall knowing that it wasn't over yet. The final test. I didn't know if I could do it but if I didn't… oh God, if I didn't, it would start all over again….

He flipped off the light and darkness filled the room. Revulsion filled every fiber of my being with a hatred I couldn't explain. I knew what was expected of me, in his arrogant offering of mercy. *I don't think I can do it. I don't think I can do this*, was the resounding scream echoing silently in my soul. *Please, don't make me*—the words I wanted to beg of him would never pass my lips. The thought reverberated and echoed into the abyss of the never spoken.

I heard the words I dreaded.

"Show me you love me."

Nausea rose in my throat. The pain coupled with that sick feeling of having to go through the final disgusting, humiliating act of penance was almost more than my stomach could hold. How could such a sacred act of covenant become so dirty, so defiled, and so repulsive? Everything lovely and pure about my womanhood was taken and used to gratify a sinful need to obtain complete submission and surrender of my soul. The very act that should always be freely given in a demonstration of love was taken, used and tossed aside as nothing.

As he drifted off to sleep, I lay there, numb with pain of soul and heart and body. Broken in a way that I didn't understand. My body was past the point of exhaustion. Terror kept me awake. Words from the past echoed in my mind,

*I've lain here and watched you sleep...wondering what it would feel like to kill you....* I listened to him breathe and waited for the remaining two hours of the night to pass.

## Chapter 2

The pain was excruciating as I lay in the bed next to this man who had pledged to always be there for me, to love me and protect me. Fear kept my eyes from closing, searing pain kept me from moving, my mind knew it wasn't over. I lay there listening to him breathe and to the rise and fall of his chest. Even in the dark, I could feel the presence of the loaded shot-gun still propped against the wall next to his head, an ever present reminder. Part of me wished I had courage to take the gun and the part of me that loved Jesus was afraid of burning in hell.

Something had shifted in the atmosphere this time. An irreversible change. A darkness, an evil that I cannot explain filled our house. It was almost as if, in the darkness of the night, I could hear an echo of supernatural laughter as evil forces circled their prey to finish off the task... to steal, kill and destroy.

A place deep in my soul had been broken, and I didn't know if I could ever put it back together again. It was that epiphany moment where time seemed to stand still as I struggled to formulate a plan, but felt as if precious moments were simply gone in a second. Before I was ready, those two short hours of remaining night had passed and soon the slumbering beast would reawaken. If I was lucky, the façade of normalcy would continue and I would devise our escape... if not, I might not see the light of another day.

My body instinctively tensed as the minutes ticked away and still I jumped when the alarm shattered the silence. A sickening fear that I cannot describe started in the recesses of my gut and quickly began to spread throughout my body. I couldn't control the trembling of my body, soul and spirit as he began to stir. Never a pleasant riser, I knew this wasn't going to be easy.

Slowly, I inched my pain ridden body to the edge of the bed to gather his work clothes and lay out a towel for his shower. The physical act of standing almost had me in a crumpled heap of brokenness on the floor. I knew the injury to my low back was serious and I was afraid that with any one step I might be paralyzed. Slowly making my way to the bathroom, I flipped on the light and shut the door. I needed a moment to gather my strength and put on the mask of submissive wife. Nearly twenty-four hours had passed since I had slept. How was I going to do all that I needed to do and survive it?

As I looked in the mirror and saw eyes swollen from crying and a face battered and scratched, my breath stuck in my throat. An unrecognizable face stared back at me. After years of assaults with hidden bruises, this face staring back at me was unexpected. The façade was shattered. How fitting that the only times my face was bruised were the very first and the very last. I stared at the stranger in the mirror and I knew that we had danced to the evil puppet master's music for the very last time. How the story would end I wasn't sure, but I had a sinking feeling that if I didn't leave that day… I wouldn't have a chance to ever dance again... at least not in this life.

I knew that I had to be cautious to play my part well this day. My very life (and maybe Amanda's) depended on it. Revulsion at the thought of what lay ahead held me captive for just a moment. I hated games and wearing masks. I wasn't sure I would be able to pull it off or that he would believe me. I felt myself on the precipice of insanity and just one small breath would shove me over into the abyss.

He was eerily quiet as he prepared for work. I let my baby girl continue to sleep even though it was time for her school bus to arrive. The middle school bus came early. As I packed his lunch, I started formulating the beginning of a plan. Would I have enough courage to carry it through? THAT I didn't know. As I teetered on that edge, my mind shifted back and forth from the paralyzing terror of leaving and the hopeless dread of staying. Somewhere in our house my keys and glasses were hidden. First things first; I had to get them back, but my timing had to be perfect.

Moving through the motions of dressing, he never mentioned the night before. His eerie silence spoke volumes. It seemed as if those periods of time were always swept away into never-never land, only spoken of in my secret prayers.

The rattle of the school bus caught my attention as it slowed in front of our house. I waited for the pause and held my breath. His voice of complaint was silent. After a hesitant moment, the bus continued its lonely, early morning journey down our road. Softly, I exhaled. It might just work.

He moved in slow motion toward the door. Following behind with his lunch in my hand, I knew I only had one shot to get it right.

"I need to take Manda to school."

Forcing myself to look him in the eye, I had to convince him there wasn't a plan. Somehow I was convinced he could see straight into my soul. I wasn't strong enough to carry on the façade for long. The abyss was widening as I stood there teetering waiting for his response. I knew he would either allow me to drive her or he would tell me to keep her home for the day. The stillness in his voice threw me off guard. He was as numb inside as I was. I felt a twinge of the familiar softening, the bond trying to re-form. I fought it back and cried inside from the loss of it.

I wasn't sure about the day, the plan, or even my next breath. I didn't know if I could pull this off. How could I be strong enough? Now, as I stood in this pivotal moment, all I had was just one moment to decide. Dare I risk it?

"Can I, please, have my glasses and car keys? She missed the bus. I can't take her to school without them."

His eyes looked deep, peering into my soul. That broken cord between us affected us both with sadness. I was sure he could read the truth written on my heart. Looking back, I think maybe he also felt the loss of what should have been. Perhaps, he was tired of the dance as well.

He went into the bedroom and handed them to me. Slowly, I stretched out my hand to take them from him, unable to see clearly, I stood there exposed and vulnerable.

He turned again toward the door and he hesitated just a moment as he looked at me. My instinct told me his heart was waiting, begging for me to ask him to stay home, to talk… to work things out. In another life, I would have, before the cord of love was severed. The pain, fear and uncertainty of the moment faded as the bittersweet reality of what I was about to do rushed over me. My happily ever after was never to be. Grief washed over me as he stood there, waiting. I couldn't explain the pain stabbing my heart. The love was gone and the sense of loss took me by surprise. The sadness I couldn't explain.

He waited a moment longer, and then as if he realized I wasn't going to ask him to stay, he looked deeply into my eyes as if he knew it was goodbye.

"Don't do me dirty today, baby."

The heavens shifted and he felt it as well.

It was never going to be the same after this moment.

As he reached down to claim his kiss, a serpent's hiss condemned me, "JUDAS!" The betrayer's kiss… But, I had no choice! I wanted to live.

I looked him the eye, praying he wouldn't see truth.

"I won't."

The lie pierced my soul and I could feel the ripping of our marriage vow. My spirit felt the rift and I knew there was no turning back.

His work boots clanked across the floor of the porch. I heard the sound of the porch door close and with it, the door to my heart closed as well. THIS TIME, there would be no returning. No second guessing, no rekindling of something long dead. Grief and numbness grappled for a moment, trying to possess my thinking.

I stood by the door, waiting and listening. The motor started and a few minutes later, a crunching sound of tires against rocks was my sign to move. Uncertainty halted my steps as I feared he might return. I half expected to hear that familiar sound again followed by a lame excuse of a forgotten item just to see if I was being true to my word.

Multiple scenarios played over in my head, and I knew there was only one chance to do it right.

It was still early, 6:30 or so on that chilly Michigan morning. Our one neighbor was my husband's close friend, and I knew he was also a spy- or so I had been told. Instinct told me to proceed with caution. One lone privacy fence separated our yard from his.

Our two houses were surrounded by the beautiful majesty of Michigan woods and pines, completely untamed and untouched by man. My stealthy, hunter mate knew them intimately and could traverse the pine covered ground silently and without notice. Even the creatures accepted him, Mother Nature went about her business as if he belonged in her midst. As I stood in the house, the woods took on another presence as if eyes were hidden and watching. Hidden in the recess, waiting. There were other nights when he had made the trek, parking his truck on the road adjacent to the edge of our woods, practicing his skills of watching while we slept, unaware in our beds.

"Manda, Get up, baby, we've got to go."

My beautiful fourteen-year old looked at me with deep soulful eyes, much too old and wise for her age.

Quickly, she scanned my face. "Let's go."

The relief was evident on her face when she realized she wouldn't have to beg me this time.

We began to scramble through the house gathering up clothes, and whatever else we would need. Totally unprepared to move, we frantically searched the house for boxes, bags, anything to hold what little we could take. Then a fear of what might be lurking just at the edge of our yard halted me in my tracks. If he saw me leave the house with a box, I would never make it out of the yard.

"Go get a couple of your back packs." She nodded and headed for her room.

It was the only thing I knew to do. I wasn't sure how I would explain TWO back packs but I would cross that bridge when I came to it.

Standing in front of the refrigerator, freezer door standing open, I counted the stash of money I had taken from his hiding place. I knew I dare not take it all because his wrath would be even greater once he found out what I had done. It didn't matter. I wasn't coming back. Peeling three twenties from the small stash, I reluctantly put the rest back. I wasn't going to risk it. He had found me before.

I moved back through the house, trying to focus on the task at hand. My mind kept shifting and changing. I changed my mind with every step. I stopped in front of my computer. It was mine. It contained my dreams and hopefully my future. Novels and book proposals tucked away, hidden in files and discs. I started to take it apart, then stopped. If he was watching, he would know.

"Mom, take your computer."

"I'm afraid to! What if he's out there and he sees? It'll be bad… so bad!"

"THEN CALL THE POLICE!" For others,

that would be the wisest choice, but they didn't know MY husband. They didn't know, like I did, what he was capable of. More scenarios, like clips from a movie that should never be, played through my mind ... The endless minutes, nearing an hour or more that it took the police to respond to an arsonist at the neighbor's house the year before... precious minutes wasted when the outcome wouldn't be good. Guilt and fear always removed my fingers from the phone dial in the past. I simply wanted to leave, to rid him of the obvious pain that my mere existence in his presence caused. The other scenes of that movie did not end well, and for me that was not an option.

Confusion, fear and lack of sleep had us both checking and watching and hurriedly trying to pack. *Hurry, hurry, hurry...* an inner voice urged me on.

Without ever having been to war, I completely understood the fear of having an unknown enemy lurking and waiting. We couldn't wait forever. I knew that time was running out and we would have to make our move for the car.

I looked around my house at my piano with ivory keys, our nameless cat, pictures of childhood and happier times, Amanda's toys, baby blankets and memories we could never replace. Then I looked at Amanda, back pack ready to go, and the decision was made.

"Okay... are you ready?" She nodded. "Let's go."

Knowing the time was now or never, we made a break for it and headed out the door. I kept reminding myself that he thought I was taking her to school. I tried to act naturally as we walked the few steps to the car. My panic was visible as I was barely able to make coherent sentences. My daughter became the voice of reason, kept me on track, and kept me moving.

Sitting behind the steering wheel was almost my undoing. The pain in my back was like nothing I had ever known. There wasn't a position that didn't hurt. Truly, I needed an ambulance and driving was not the best idea, but I didn't see any other way for us to get to safety.

My religion taught me that leaving my husband was a mortal sin. My heart told me I didn't have a choice. I was torn between religion and life. I didn't understand how a merciful God could require such a sacrifice from me. Above all else, I wanted to please my God. I wanted to do what was right. I hated being put in this position. I raged at a God who would do this to His child.

*****

Hoping for help and trying to ease my guilt, I decided to take a chance and hope that she could make it stop. Amanda glared at me in disbelief as I drove the few miles to my mother-in-law's apartment.

She was the voice of God in our world. I needed answers. I needed spiritual approval to leave. Our religion was harsh and full of rules that felt impossible to meet. I feared burning in a fiery hell for leaving my husband. I tried to be a martyr, my life for his, but I wasn't strong enough. I couldn't do it. I just couldn't.

We pulled into the visitor parking area of the apartment complex. I took a deep breath as I stepped out of my car. Amanda glared at me from her side of the car.

"She's not going to help us, Mom. You already know that. She's just going to call him and tell him where we are."

"I'm not going to tell her where we are going. I have to do this, Manda. I have to give her the chance to do the right thing."

Amanda rolled her brown eyes at me and trudged, reluctantly, behind me toward her grandmother's door.

Waking her from a sound sleep with our knocking, she warily let us in. She had been down this road before with me and with others.

"Amanda, will you go and wait in the other room please." Amanda tossed a look my direction that showed me clearly what she thought about that request but she did as I asked.

I wanted to protect her heart toward her father. I didn't want her to hear details of the night.

"We are going to a shelter. I can't do this anymore." I shared with her some of the details of what had taken place the night before. She listened in stony silence without speaking a word.

Amanda, impatient with waiting in the other room alone, returned near the end of my story. I looked up at my daughter and wasn't surprised at the look of disgust on her face as she realized her grandmother's reaction.

"Grandma, look at Mom's FACE!" The room was still shrouded in darkness, blinds closed and lights off except for a hall light shining from the edge of the room. Pulling her robe tighter around her, a pained expression on her face, she lifted her hand toward the lamp on the end table next to her. I watched her arm move as if in slow motion. Arm stopping in midair, she made the conscious decision in that moment to choose her side. Her own past and demons were hers to face. In that moment I prayed for her soul because her blood, her DNA had done this to me. I watched in disbelief, as her arm dropped back into her lap, just before reaching the pull for the lamp.

From the shadows where she was sitting, lamp still shrouded in darkness, her voice crackled but grew firmer in determination, "I don't see a thing." Her arm falling limp in her lap.

Oh the curse of the generations. It does not lie in the reward of the forgiven heart. The curse lies in the reverberating consequence of the ancestor's unrepentant heart. The selfish flesh, full of transgressions, oh how they affect their children, and their children's children in words, hurts, rejection, abandonment, denial and all of those things evil that would steal our souls from God. Those tiny cords connecting us together, in good or evil, generation to generation can be so strong some may never break free. Sadness overwhelmed me as I looked at this widow, sitting alone on her couch, this woman, held by her own tiny cords.

Amanda and I both stared at her in hurt and shock. I was immediately sorry I had come. I was sorry I had expected her to do the right thing. I was sorry I had been a part of this family for so many years. With the anger finally starting to burn inside me for the injustices throughout the years, I looked at her with my own disgust spewing from my voice, "I'm sorry to have bothered you. We are going to a shelter."

"I don't want to know anything else. I don't want to know where you're going."

"Not a problem." Manda looked as if she wanted to say to her grandmother, and I was afraid in her anger she would say something we both would regret. I herded her out the door and we made our way back to the car. That move could have cost me. If he had come back home, he was only a phone call and minutes away. We had to move!

One more stop before the exodus could begin. I located the store front in the small strip mall quickly and ran up to the door with pen and paper in hand. The stillness of the morning, in our quiet town, was yet unbroken as we passed through the shopping district long before the changing of factory shifts and business doors unlocking for the day. I had been to this place years before, this Center for Women in Transition. It was a satellite office. The door was locked and lights turned out. No help from this office today. We would need to go to their main office instead. Jotting down the phone number and address, I raced back to the car.

We still had a drive ahead of us to get to the

women's center, but first we had to make it out of our town. The streets were silent, except for the occasional, lone passing car. It was an odd, disconcerting feeling, an odd vulnerability, driving exposed, unprotected from watching eyes. Oh the safety of hiding in the open when surrounded by noises of life and busy people.

We traveled a two lane highway and witnessed as we passed empty cornfields, old farmhouses and the beauty of Michigan landscape in the spring. With every mile behind us, I began to hope that maybe, just maybe, we might really have a chance to be safe. Squirming in the seat, I forced myself to keep driving. With no comfortable position, pain radiated in needle-like waves up my spine.

As we neared the quaint town of Holland, nestled on the shore of Lake Michigan, I felt my panic rise again. Being unfamiliar with the streets and layout of the roads my knowledge of navigating this city was limited. Tulips lined the streets in dignified glory, resplendent in neat and colorful rows. In just a few short weeks, their admirers would arrive from around the world.

At the first gas station I could find, we went in to find a map and something to drink. Counting out change, for a payphone in the parking lot, I called the number I had written on the paper from a payphone in the parking lot. The hotline worker gave me directions to the center's office and off we were again.

The parking lot was empty at the domestic violence center. Warily, we settled in for the wait. In my exhaustion, I struggled to reason through what might lay ahead for us. I nervously eyed the road in both directions scared that he would fly into the parking lot in a rage at any moment. I prayed he would head in the opposite direction from our home toward Kalamazoo to look for me.

The obstacles were almost more than I could stand. I had no earthly idea where our help would come from or if it would come at all. Bridges burned, from times gone by, made people tired of helping. Dark, sinister, cords of failure and shame kept me in my previous escape. The problem—I had run out of people to call. Those tiny, invisible cords were woven around my heart and held me captive in their grip.

How does life come to this point, this place where the crossroad reached has no signs? We live in a world so full of beauty and hope, yet somehow that day we had found ourselves running in fear for our lives. Destiny's cruel sense of humor, the irony of life. In any direction one could think to travel, friends, family and foe, and still I stood at the crossroad, unsure, unsafe and alone.

*Memories of another escape seared into my soul and formed a deep, painful scar. As I fled to the yard, I couldn't go back. My heart, my child, was still inside. His presence blocked the door. If I went back inside, I might never leave again and the brutality of the last attack still had me reeling to recover. My heart trusted that the bond between father and child would protect her from his anger. My soul believed his wrath would not touch her. I alone was the target of his hatred. If I had known the plot whispered in his ear, I would have boldly gone back through the door and taken whatever fate I may. The torment of weeks to come sent me reeling into a darkness of despair, as my precious heart was dangled tauntingly before me, making me dance to the master's tune, stripping me of dignity and will. The blackmail of heart and soul saying I had forsaken her and willingly left her to his devices went against everything I stood for, but I had no defense, no proof, and no witnesses. I was brave and strong and broken for a fragment of time until she was delivered back to me. The constant threat hung heavy in the air that it would take but a moment for her to disappear, never to be seen again. I would never make that mistake again.*

Fear was written in the seriousness of Amanda's brow and I recognized the blood coursing through her veins as a defiance sparked in her eyes—a defiance I had seen before from older yet similar eyes.

"We can't go back, Mom. I don't care where we live. I'd rather live in the car than go back." I knew she was right, but I could hear that distant threat echoing through time, reminding me not to forget.

Nine in the morning couldn't come fast enough. We sat and waited for someone to open the door. I kept willing them to open early. I wanted them to hurry and fix it for me, to make it all stop. I was so tired. Every ounce of my being cried out for sleep. The pain in my back wouldn't stop. How much more, God? How much is one person supposed to take?

Finally, after an eternity of waiting, I watched as a woman unlocked the door. Cautiously, we made that journey from the car to the door. The whole thing was very surreal. The trauma from the entire nightmare had my head in a fog. It was hard to tell what was real and what wasn't. It felt like a bad horror movie. As much as we wanted out of it there was no escaping. How did my life, with all my hopes and dreams, end up in this shambles?

I approached the counter and the receptionist asked me to take a seat and fill out some papers. The wall of plate glass windows facing the parking lot left me feeling exposed and vulnerable to the world.

"Is there someplace else we could wait?

Please?" Her expression never changed. "I called the hotline. I'm the one that called earlier. My husband's looking for me."

She seemed totally unconcerned about our danger. I wanted to scream. I wanted out of that lobby. The door was unlocked. He could walk in the door at any moment. My back was screaming and felt on fire. Shifting my weight from side to side in the uncomfortable lobby chair, I struggled to complete the paperwork.

Eventually I finished and handed it to the receptionist. A few moments later, she called us to follow her back and down a hallway. The small office was pristine and neat. Everything was in its place. Soon, a woman came in to join us. She was petite, stout, with hair cropped in an efficient cut. Her simple, business attire was of a neutral pallet and blended into the neutrality of the office décor.

"Hi, my name is Jan and I'm here to get some information and see how we can help."

As she settled into the chair beside me, I felt annoyed at her pace, not hurried, as if we had all the time in the world. Her manner of speech matched her gait: slow, steady and deliberate in tone. It was aggravating and comforting at the same time.

"Can you tell me what happened?" She asked in that smooth, expressionless voice, and I completely lost it. The pressure cooker exploded, and I sobbed hysterically for what felt like an eternity. No matter how hard I tried, I could not pull myself together. Minutes passed before words would form in my mouth. The breaking point had been reached.

All the years of betrayal, hurt, abuse, infidelity, lies, and broken promises just bubbled up and over and the dam broke. The fear. Oh my God, the FEAR! It never went away. Every single day, even in my sleeping hours, I was afraid. The horror of the night before, begging for my life, the threats, my injury, the past. The stinking, horrible past. Being tied up, beaten, yelled at, and cursed. All of it just came flooding out. All of the secrets and the lies covering up the abuse, I couldn't hold it anymore. She handed me an endless supply of tissues as it all came flooding out.

Finally able to talk, I stood and paced the room trying to get comfortable and relieve the wretched pain in my back. It was relentless — the throbbing, pulsating pain, made focusing on details nearly impossible.

"You need to be seen by a doctor. There is a hospital nearby. Will you let one of us drive you or call you an ambulance?" Fear and panic took over again. A million, crazed questions flooded my mind: Could I trust them? I didn't know these people. What if they called the police on me? What if they turned me in to CPS because I was homeless? I had stayed. OH DEAR GOD, why did I stay so long? Would that count against me?

I didn't want to leave my car, afraid he would find it and take it. The thought of a stranger taking me to the hospital was intimidating. I didn't want them in my business. I didn't want to be a burden. Help was not something I was used to. Trust was not something I extended, because every time I did, it betrayed me!

After much convincing, I finally agreed to go and get checked out.

"That's all right... I can drive. I can make it." After I surrendered and gave my word, Jan issued a dire warning—"If you truly don't want the police involved, please know that if the doctor or staff believes you or your daughter are in danger, they may notify the police." Those sobering words almost made me change my mind, but the pain was worse and I needed assistance walking. I had no idea how I was going to be able to look for work, or even take care of simple business. I could barely move. There were so many decisions to make, so much to sort through. It was simply too much.

"Please, check back in with us after you get checked out." I hastily agreed. I needed their help. I had no place else to go. She continued on with her instructions. I retained what I could and wrote down the rest. I wasn't sure I would remember any of it by sundown.

"Our shelter is full right now." I felt a sinking feeling in the pit of my stomach. What had I done? I hadn't even considered that they wouldn't have room for us. It was an emergency shelter. We were having an emergency. I was floored. I began to panic again. "But, we may have a room come open tomorrow." she assured me. "We have someone who is supposed to be moving out tomorrow. As soon as she does, the room is yours. For tonight, there's a brand new homeless shelter for women and children here in town. It's a great facility. They have room for you to stay tonight. If you can go there, we will see what we can do tomorrow."

The staff continued to try to convince me to let them call an ambulance but I was too foolishly embarrassed to ride in an ambulance. I was also afraid Amanda wouldn't be able to ride with me if I did. I didn't want to be separated from her. I was afraid someone would take her away from me. I would rather not go to the hospital at all than risk losing her. They gave me a folder of paperwork and directions to the homeless shelter and helped me get back into my car.

We were all we had. I clung to her and her

to me. The Lone Ranger and Tonto. No matter what it took, I had to make sure she was safe. He couldn't get his hands on her. Whatever the cost, I was willing to pay it.

Seasons in life are amazing things: the roads traveled, lessons learned, and people met. Some contain new life, joy, happiness and peace while others contain great sorrow and pain. Upon each season the stage is set with timing, the set and the actors. How like life to be that dramatic, with unscripted stories created from the beginning of time, cast down through the seasons with twists and turns as the centuries old conflict continues, that battle between good and evil. Behind those scenes lie another tale, journey, road and story with each one intricately woven together to play a role in time.

My season was changing, a shifting of scene and cast. The lessons learned would write the chapters for the stage now looming before me. With every step were choices that would determine the coming set for my season. Feeling the weight of eternity resting on what I would choose, I struggled to make doing what was "right" a priority at all cost. Painful decisions and choices would impact how future seasons would be played for generations to come.

## Chapter 3

As the morning progressed and minutes continued to pass, my heart and my reasoning collided. Thoughts contradicted each other, memories were hard to recall, and emotions spiraled out of control and tears... so many tears. Every step and every decision felt like another betrayal. The evil beauty, the sinister irony was that betrayal played both sides. "It's all your fault." came the hissing serpent again, taunting me. "YOU did this. No one is ever going to love you... now...." The puppet master's hand at work. With every word spoken he was entangling another cord of control. How sly and cunning his trickery. How smooth the dance continues, that pulling of a cord, and the characters on the stage begin their waltz, in perfection rhythm, in unity of time. The stage, not confined to human time and space, expanding as the characters are played, his greedy need for power enticing him to pull the cords... to make the puppets dance.

Reluctantly, we made our way to the hospital. I was half afraid Amanda would blurt it all out in order for us to receive help. So many years of praying for rescue in the middle of the storm, without fail and to no avail, had almost convinced me that I was beyond help. Unworthy. I was afraid to believe that hope had finally arrived. Fear is a powerful captor.

Hurtful, remembered words sliced liked a powerful sword straight to the core of my being, day after day, year after year until everything inside of me was shredded and shrouded in a curse of lies. The thought of finally speaking up and speaking truth was almost more than I could do. How do I profess the criminal acts against me when inside I was convinced it was all my fault? Confusion of thought and reason pulled and tugged and caused the lies to form.

"So, can you tell me how this injury happened?" the triage nurse asked.

I shot Amanda a warning look, before I answered.

"My husband and I were goofing around and fell off the bed. He landed on top of me and when he did I heard and felt something pop in my back"—I prayed for forgiveness before the words were out. She made her notations on the computer and continued with her assessment. Soon we were taken back to a treatment room and we waited for the doctor to examine me.

"Mom, you need to tell the truth."

"I'm scared to. Your dad will lose his mind if he gets arrested. What if they call CPS because I didn't leave and they take you away from me? I don't want to make this worse."

I wiggled and moved from side to side on the exam table trying to find a comfortable position. Nothing worked. I inched my way off the bed and paced the room. Eventually, I tried leaning across the bed. The pain was excruciating.

Eventually the doctor came into our exam room and repeated the nurse's questions. I repeated the same story. He gave me a skeptical look and I knew he didn't believe me. As we waited for x-rays and other tests to come back, I anxiously anticipated police officers or my husband to enter our cubicle.

"Well we have the results of your X-ray. It appears to be normal. It appears to be either a torn ligament or muscle in your back. You will need to follow up with your family doctor if it doesn't get any better for additional tests. Do you have a driver today?"

He looked from me to Amanda.

"No. It's just us."

"Well, I can give you a shot for pain but you would need someone to drive you."

"I don't have anyone I can call."

"All right then. I'll give you a prescription for pain medication to help you get through until you go see your family doctor."

The oral pain medication they had given me helped ease it enough so that I could drive a little more comfortably. I was grateful, for we still had a LONG day ahead.

We followed the map the center had given us to get to the homeless shelter. Amanda and I both felt a different kind of fear. The only shelters we had ever seen were on television. We weren't homeless people. I owned a house that was full of memories, presents and our life. I worked in banking and retail. I didn't understand HOW I had gotten to this point? How had this happened? I didn't get it. It was as if I had been living my life through the deceptive haze of a fog. My truth was a distorted reality. Then suddenly the fog was lifted away and the scenery around me shifted and changed before my eyes. My world, my season, was nothing like I had thought. What a cruel joke to play. I wanted the game to be over. Ha-ha. You got me. But, it wasn't a game. It was real and our lives were at stake.

The building was brand new but it looked like a hospital. We walked inside to the lobby area and spoke with the receptionist who was expecting us. She barely looked up as she handed me the clipboard. Another packet of paperwork to fill out. A list of shelter rules. It felt like the 100th time I had shared my story that day. I started to feel less than human and definitely invisible as I moved through the shelter processes.

She led us down a hall to a closet area where she gave us army blankets, pillows, sheets, towels and toiletries. "New" doesn't necessarily mean "cozy" or "warm" or "inviting." The halls were sterile and so was the staff. It was an institution.

She unlocked a door and ushered us into the room we were to share hopefully just for one night. The room was stark and bare. Inside were two army style metal bunk beds with army style mattresses. I wasn't sure sleeping would be an option in that bed, based on the amount of pain radiating from my back.

"You have to be out of here by 6:00 a.m. and you have to stay off the property until evening." I looked at her as if she had grown two heads and spoken in a foreign language.

"What are we supposed to do during the day?"

"Well, people look for work, they go to the library, find things to do. Those are the rules."

"But, I have a back injury, I can barely stand up and we are scared for our lives."

"Well, you can sit out front in the lobby during the day, but you can't be here in the room. We lock the doors."

Amanda began to cry. I could sense Amanda's panic. I felt it too.

"Can we have a few minutes?" The "warden" nodded and walked out.

"Momma, I can't do this." She kept repeating it over and over. I hugged her tight and we both cried. "I'd rather sleep in the car than do this." She was almost as tall as me but she was still my baby.

"I know baby, I don't think I can do this either. Don't worry… I'm not going to make you do this. We'll figure something else out." My mind started searching for a solution. I had to figure something out. I started adding up the money left out of the $60.00 I had brought us. After paying for gas, prescriptions and food, there wasn't much left. I didn't know what we were going to do.

We gathered up all of the items we had carried into the room with us and marched back down the hall. Back at the reception desk, I laid the items down. "We can't do this. My daughter's been through enough. I'm not making her do this." The receptionist looked at me as if I had lost my mind.

I turned around and walked out. Arms and legs trembling with exhaustion, pain and fear, I was starting to wonder if this nightmare "day from hell" would ever end. In defeat, I turned our car back towards the crisis center. Right before closing, I forced myself to go back inside. I hate being one of those "on your last nerve" kind of people, but that day I didn't have a choice. I was running out of options.

"Would it be possible to make a long distance call? I will pay you for it, if I need to."

"We aren't allowed to let anyone make long distance calls."

"Please, can you ask someone if just this once you make an exception? I need to call my mom. She's on vacation in Georgia. Please?"

At the moment, if the answer had come back "no," I think it would have been the final straw. I think my mind would have simply snapped and I would have just given up. Game over. Well played. I surrender.

However, they took me back to that little office space again, put in a code to dial out on the phone, and within minutes I was sharing what had happened with my mom.

"Mom," —I couldn't stop the tears—"Amanda and I are in Holland trying to get into the shelter. He beat me up again but they don't have any openings. Can I borrow some money?"

"You can go and stay at my apartment. You have a key."

"I can't go there. That's the first place he'll go to look for us. It's bad this time. He really hurt me. Can you loan me a couple hundred? I'll pay you back as soon as I get back on my feet."

"That's fine. You're a signer on the checking account."

"Okay. There's a branch not far from here. Thank you."

I felt sure the crisis center staff was completely annoyed that I kept bothering them all day, but they were my life line. Without them I was destined to sink and quickly drown. I was done. Completely done. It had been thirty-four hours since I had slept.

We drove back to the area of town I was somewhat familiar with, checked into a Budget 8 Motel, ordered pizza for delivery and clicked the lock on the door. As soon as that door shut, and we were safe inside with the world locked out, we could finally relax and I could breathe again. As the fear began to subside, showers were taken and with pajamas on, we spent the next few hours watching senseless television.

Relief overwhelmed me as we both lay in our own beds. Amanda flipped the channels while I lay there mindlessly watching the screen. Years upon years of pent up fear slipped away in just one night of not having to worry about a fight. I was just too tired to fight anymore. I was thankful that I could sleep without praying my nightly prayer, "Father, please, set a watch before my mouth tonight," afraid that I would have a dream and say something in my sleep that would cause me to get hurt. That fear had always kept me from sleeping soundly. No need to worry about a senseless argument turning into an all-night ordeal.

There was so much to sift through in my mind. The loyalty I felt toward this man made no sense. Constantly, I kept defending and downplaying all that had happened. It had become part of my routine. Part of the cover up. To hide the secrets. To give guilt and shame free reign to manipulate truth. My heart wanted his heart to be okay. In my twisted concept of truth, I wanted him to be happy and to go on about his life but to just let me go. Release me from the prison of that season. So many thoughts drifting through my mind. Quickly, exhaustion released me from my tormented thoughts and I fell into a deep, healing sleep.

The rays of the morning sun peeked through the curtains and woke me. I looked over at my sleeping daughter and was so grateful she was safe. She was with me. We were going to be okay. We had to be.

We ate left over pizza for breakfast, watched some more television and stayed in the room until the last possible moment. Part of me wished we could just stay there in that room without coming out. We could hide and the world would not be able to find us, but I knew that was definitely not possible. Reluctantly, we packed our clothes and cleaned up the room.

Before leaving I used the phone to call the hotline at the center and let them know where we were.

"I'm glad you called. Our lady hasn't moved out yet but we may have a bed open in our other shelter. The room should be ready later today."

I felt a sense of relief. "I'll take it."

Then she named the town.

"That's where we live." That familiar sense of panic began to wash over me again as the cords began to stretch and pull, calling the players back to the dance floor.

"If you think you can do it, you can stay there just until the room here opens up and then we'll transfer you back here." The sense of relief from the night before was gone. The brief flicker of hope was still there, kindling in the back of my mind: at least we would have a bed. If we could just get to the shelter, we could stay inside and he couldn't hurt us.

"We'll do it."

"Okay… check in with us later and I'll let you know when you can drive over."

The daylight hours loomed in front of us with unforgiving sunshine and happiness around us. Another long agonizing day with no place to go. No one to share our horror with. Feeling like no one really even cared. We drove around town and took in the sights and then worked our way back to the mall and sat in the parking lot for several hours. As darkness began to fall once again, we called the hotline to check in. The room would be ready by the time we got there. We couldn't believe that in less than 48 hours we were headed back down that same lonely stretch of highway.

Nervous hands gripped the steering wheel as our black Park Avenue silently purred its way back to the place we feared. Every shadow on the road, every flash of light made us jump. Tension rose the closer we came to the place we had called home for so many years. The only school Amanda had ever attended, our church, our family, our life… it was all right there… the places we could see and touch, but it almost felt as if we were invisible to it all. In this new season, we didn't fit. We no longer belonged. My heart was distant from this place. It was a place of endings.

Cautiously, we inched our way through town, Saturday night was not the night we wanted to be in our hometown. Amanda was on high alert for any sign of that familiar truck we both hated with a passion. Never one to remember street names, I started to panic a little, as I began following the specific instructions to the shelter. The familiar roads were leading us to a dangerous place. It didn't take but another turn for us to realize that it could ALL be over in just a moment, as the road took us directly in front of the friend's house where he spent the majority of his non-working time.

I was starting to doubt that I would ever be free. My humanity had become consumed by ownership to this controlling master. Nothing was my own, not even my will to live or die. I had no say in it. My voice was hidden behind the mask of submission. It was as if this great tug of war for life had become a vicious game, and the outcome would depend on the ultimate power of those cords, those strings that had more control over me than just my will to survive. Some of those cords were stronger than others, some caused tremendous pain. Others we could not even feel their hold, at times.

The evilness of the game dated back generations where others had taken this stage before us. One might think that those whispered moments of painful recollection, that familiar sense that you have seen this before in your dreams, would be enough to awaken the strength to break free and yet one would underestimate the power of the deceiver.

That nagging, sinister voice whispering again, "You didn't have to do this. You could have just stayed at YOUR house, in YOUR bed... none of this would be happening right now if you hadn't left. He loves you... he would do anything for you... why would you hurt him like this?" Guilt, blame, shame, lies, deception... tugging on those cords, pulling them, manipulating... all a game... a vicious game to hurt us all. This evil tormenter of families proclaimed no one a winner in the vast scheme of things. Everyone would pay a price.

It was a normal house, on a normal street. Other houses nestled on either side with normal families on the inside watching television, eating dinner, preparing for bed. How could a normal world continue to exist and go on about their normal way, when passing through, past their front door, on their street, was the hunted? The prey. It was a sick, surreal moment to pass that house. Quickly scanning the drive and street, we saw no sign of that hated truck. Our journey continued to a destination just a few blocks away. Thankfully, we were blessed NOT to know, at that moment in time, that he had gotten a rental car to conduct his hunt for us.

It was dark pulling up to the shelter. The building wasn't what we expected but it certainly looked safe. If we could stay inside the walls. The door opened and the shelter worker let us in. We were expected. We could smell something cooking on the stove.

"Come on in and have a seat."

I collapsed in a chair at the table.

"I don't think we can stay here." I explained to the worker about the house, on the road—the only road that led to the shelter. We couldn't stay inside forever. We would have to eventually leave. Amanda couldn't stay in her same school. It wouldn't be safe for either of us. He would take her. He would find our car. He would find the shelter. I would be dead. Quickly she got on the phone to the main office once she realized that our being there could jeopardize the lives of everyone in that house. It was quickly apparent that they needed to act quickly and get us out of there.

Finally, the heavens had mercy and while we were speaking the room opened up at the other shelter. The woman was packing and leaving. They would clean the room and prepare for our arrival. Thank God. I couldn't take much more. She herded us quickly back to the car as if at any moment we would be discovered, and I knew that her worries had merit. I knew if I could just make it past that house and that part of town, we should be able to dodge main roads and get back out of town... back to the land of tulips. The last hours of that day we spent driving dark roads, avoiding the places we knew he might be. All the while never knowing we were watching for the wrong vehicle. That, my friends, was grace.

Once again, following instructions in the dark unfamiliar area was rather daunting, but it was much preferable to the alternative. The directions took us down a long, dark road that seemed to go on forever. I began to doubt that I had followed the directions correctly. One more small turn to the right, and we were on a residential road at the very shore's edge of the majestic Lake Michigan. Certainly we had taken a wrong turn. She promised the porch light would be on at the door, and amazingly it was. The shadowed light lit up the numbers that matched what was written on the directions in my lap. Warily, I pulled into the driveway still afraid it couldn't be true. This beautiful two story, brick, lakefront home could not possibly be our safe haven. We sat in the car and stared at the house, afraid the owners would make us leave.

The front door opened and a college-aged woman clad in sweat pants and t-shirt beckoned to us from the door. That was our cue. We looked at each other and smiled. We made it.

## Chapter 4

After two days of living on the run, our hearts needed a quiet place to mend. As we walked through the front door into the foyer, neither of us could believe that we were actually going to be living in this beautiful home. It was as if our souls were granted an amazing gift that we could not comprehend. The shelter the day before had been an institution. This was a home.

The foyer opened up into an open-concept kitchen / living / dining room area furnished with a large dining table and the cozy living room had deep, rich wood built-in cabinets. It was the perfect room to cuddle up with a book or to watch a movie. The spacious kitchen was furnished with every appliance imaginable and fully-equipped for cooking. It was warm and inviting. Downstairs were two bathrooms, a laundry room, and an office. Off the back of the house was a huge deck and hot tub. Although there were houses on either side, there were no houses behind. The back yard was private and secluded and opened into undeveloped land, wooded and filled with Michigan pines.

The upstairs was open-concept, and the landing had railing all the way around offering a view to the downstairs. It was all beautifully furnished and nicer than anything we had ever lived in. We were shown to our room, and just a flicker of hope flared in my heart. It was so comforting to have our own room. We needed it more than words could say. I believe that this house was timed just for us. Thankful that their actual shelter was being renovated and they had rented this lovely summer lake house located just a short walk down a path to the shore. We realized it was going to be an amazing place to heal. A place to share our hearts. A place to shut the door and escape the world. Also upstairs were, two additional bedrooms for two other families, broken and ravaged by the same vicious game.

We found comfort among the other residents. This common bond, a cord of understanding resonated throughout us all. It brought healing and security for all who bound themselves to it. The sound of laughter and tears late into the night and the wee hours of the morning was a beckoning call to the dining room for a late night cup of coffee. From time to time, the sound of weeping could be heard through the walls at night. All of our hearts would collectively cry out in recognition of that hateful force that drove others to want to destroy us.

Our first night there set the stage for many evenings to come. We heard laughter coming from downstairs and the sound of it was contagious. We couldn't help but be drawn to it. Another resident worked second shift and was unwinding with her daughter at the table while she ate her late night dinner. We silently joined them at the table. I watched this robust woman sitting at the table after working a long shift and her whole demeanor was upbeat, positive and funny. I watched her in awe and couldn't understand how she could find anything to laugh about considering her situation.

The following day, the day worker came to find me.

"Mary, could you come into the office please?"

The serious tone of her voice scared me. Something was going on and it didn't sound like it was good.

"We've been getting calls on the hotline from a woman asking for you by name. She claims that she is from your doctor's office and she's trying to locate you for medical reasons."

"I haven't spoken to my doctor's office. That sounds like something my sister-in-law would do."

"We won't release any of your information. You don't have to worry about that. We've also received several calls from the Michigan State Police. The Trooper is threatening to subpoena our records to find out if you are here. If they do that we will be required to release the information. It could also jeopardize the confidentiality of everyone else here in the house as well."

*I was terrified.*

"Why are they looking for me?"

"Well, it's pretty common for an abuser to claim all kinds of things in order to locate a spouse. A lot of times they claim that they just want to make sure their children are in a safe place. If you don't talk to him, they will get a subpoena. You can use my cell phone if you want so the shelter number won't show up on caller I.D."

I called the number the officer had given her.

"Ms. Clemons, there have been allegations made of abuse toward your daughter."

"What do you mean? Abuse by ME?"

"Yes, ma'am. We need to meet with you and your daughter as soon as possible."

"All right…."

A meeting was scheduled at the main office of the crisis center.

Never had I been in trouble for anything. I was stunned. I would never harm Amanda. I adored her. She was my world. I would gladly lay down my life for her. How could he claim such a thing? My head and my heart were reeling. His hateful call started a year-long string of events that snowballed right up until the very end.

Police investigations, interviews and court hearings. Each and every day, it felt like some new hurdle had to be overcome. My heart would just begin to stop the emotional hemorrhaging and he would come up with another scheme to hurt me. As the insanity increased, new players joined the stage of this drama and their forces joined with mine. The two of us no longer alone in the dance, the new forces brought with them light to expose the hidden strings of the puppet master. Unexpected allies formed and a strong force waged war on death.

Jan drove us to the crisis center office in the shelter van. The pain in my body was still intense and coupled with trauma of all that had happened. Break-downs came over me with an intensity that took my breath away. I struggled to hold it together. Not knowing what was going to happen, I was afraid to bring Amanda, but I had no choice. My heart was afraid they would take her away and make her go back to that place.

Jan took Amanda to one room to wait and left me in a cozy sitting room. Obviously, the crisis center staff was used to this type of meeting. It wasn't long before two starkly different men entered the room. One a mousy non-descript man. He was an investigator for CPS. The other was a tall, red-headed Michigan State Police Trooper, Scott Ernstes. Both of them were stern and to the point. My heart was beating against my chest, and I had no idea what to think.

The intensity of the interview left me emotionally spent. I couldn't believe my husband could stoop so low. More guilt and more shame, layer upon layer, added to my pain. The game of cat and mouse was just beginning.

Oh, the lows that one can go to when control and power is lost. The lies, deception and manipulation, in a wicked guise to pull the prey back into the web, a web of destruction. An abyss of darkness seemed to invade every aspect of our lives. It would seem that once again, the stage was being set for another shift, another waltz, another day. The master named Control was not finished yet. His insatiable desire for power and revenge would be sated by nothing less than absolute destruction of the puppets he controlled. However, this time, the puppet master had underestimated the other players who had entered the stage. He had become arrogant in his attempts to destroy.

Accusations were hurled that totally knocked me to my knees in despair. I was unprepared for the brutality of his assault on me and everything I stood for. As I began to reach out for support, I quickly found out that every single person in my family had been contacted and told stories. Ministers all over the state had been contacted as well. The goal was to effectively cut off anyone who might have been inclined to help me.

I knew that this time there was no going back. I had to pour out details of the abuse on paper and file for a protective order in court. The shelter provided a legal advocate to assist me with filling out the paperwork.

"Just be honest and tell what happened. I can't fill out the paperwork for you but I can help you to understand the questions."

I stared at the paperwork, knowing I desperately needed this piece of paper, yet I was almost more afraid of the ramifications of getting it than not. I wanted him to leave me alone. I wanted to be free, but I was scared of increasing his anger toward me. I looked at the little box that asked the court to restrict him from carrying fire arms. I was terrified to check that box. I didn't want him to be able to carry one of his many guns. However, hunting was his life. It was the one thing he looked forward to, above all else, every year. I was scared to take that away from him. I didn't want to take that away from him, I just wanted to be safe. I knew what his reaction would be, even before the judge signed the papers. Slowly, I checked the box. I had no other choice.

Finally I had the paperwork completed and Jan drove me to the courthouse. She was familiar with the process and walked with confidence through the courthouse. I lagged behind her, unsure if I was doing the right thing.

We sat and waited for what felt like hours to see if the judge would sign the order. The day was almost through. Court was about to recess for the day. Thankfully, finally, it was done. Granted. Relief and fear, all wrapped into one. That was only step one of the process. Next I had to figure out how to have the papers served to him. It wouldn't go into effect until he was legally served, and the court didn't handle that part.

A few days later we met with the police and CPS again. This time Amanda was interviewed on camera. My heart was in shreds and my nerves were completely destroyed. To a family who claimed family was everything, I could not wrap my mind around the extremes they were willing to go to in order to protect one but sacrifice another.

The cords of the puppet master continued to pull and tug. The scenes of this horrific tale continued to shift and change as each decision made, good or evil, affected the next scene. Everyone had choices to make, and every choice had a reverberating effect.

No evidence of abuse was ever discovered by my hand, but a lot was disclosed about him. I was mortified. Trooper Ernstes brought Manda back into the room so we could all visit. I was totally oblivious to investigation tactics. I had never been in any kind of trouble with the police.

"Will you take a polygraph?" the investigating officer asked me with a stern look. "We asked your husband as well."

"Anytime! Just tell me when and where." I had nothing to hide. There was nothing else that I could share that would be any more humiliating than what I had already experienced. I just wanted it to be over.

He nodded, but seemed somewhat taken aback that I had agreed so easily. After Amanda's interview, his entire demeanor toward us changed. He softened his way of dealing with us. I was grateful. I had no way to prove that my words were true. The secrets. The lies. The blackmail. How was I ever supposed to unravel it all and be believed? How could I make them understand all of the things I didn't understand myself?

"I'll serve the protective order paperwork to him. I need to go and follow up with him anyway."

"Thank you! That would help a lot. I don't have money to pay a process server."

"Not a problem." He stood up from the table and started to wrap up our meeting. "If you want to go back to your house to get some more of your things, I'll go with you. I have time," Trooper Ernstes offered.

I knew I couldn't go back to that house without a police escort. I was so relieved. We only had a little bit of our clothing. There was so much more we needed.

Nausea rose in my throat and I struggled to maintain my composure as we made our way to the vehicles. We rode with Jan in the shelter van, and he escorted us from the child advocacy center back to our house. Every rational thought in my head screamed, "Don't go back to that place."

Everything was eerily still as we pulled into the driveway. His truck was nowhere to be seen. Going up to the door cautiously, I tried my key in the lock. The locks had all been changed, of course. That was all I needed as an excuse to walk away.

"This is still your property as much as it is his. You have a legal right to gain entry into your home."

Another decision to make that left me frozen in fear — to gain entry to the house or walk away. This was my one and only chance to get more of our things. Breaking a window was out of the question. Many lessons from the past flashed through my mind, trying to defend myself and the repercussions. It wasn't in me to fight back. I knew better.

"I always left the kitchen window unlocked because I kept it open quite a bit. Can I go check to see if it's still unlocked?"

The look on his face made it clear he wasn't thrilled with the idea of leaving the front of the house where he could see what was happening by the road but he reluctantly followed me around the side of the house and to the back of our property. He was clearly uncomfortable leaving the road side of the property, but he was trying to make sure I was safe.

"I can't physically help you in any way get into your house." He looked at the block foundation under the mobile home and he looked at me and he got a twinkle in his eye that I kind of resented. I looked at my long skirt, the foundation that was almost to my waist, the window I had to climb up to, and then the old trailer windows that cranked out from inside. This wasn't going to be dignified nor pretty, but it had to be done.

I found a bucket to climb up on, I hiked up my skirt (in as lady-like fashion as my one hundred eighty pound, out of shape, housebound body could muster) and precariously balanced on the foundation ledge. I reached through the window to try and crank it open enough to climb through. There was absolutely no possible way for grace to be a part of this scenario. I looked first at the window and then at him. He tried to cover a smile as he turned his back toward me to give me some dignity with my hiked up dress. He clearly could see my predicament. There was no way I could possibly go in feet first. I had no choice but to put my head in first and then try to figure out how to get my feet inside behind me. Halfway through the window I realized that I was going to have to fall to the floor inside. There was nothing to break my fall. Humiliated, I hit the floor with a thud. I heard something that sounded like male laughter, quickly covered up and stifled. I lay on the kitchen floor in utter humiliation.

"Hurry and go unlock the door. Don't go anywhere else in the house until I make sure it is clear." I heard his order very distinctly through the window. I raced to unlock the door. Emotion flooded through me. I wasn't at all expecting this sense of loss.

He searched the house room by room before giving us the go ahead to get our stuff. "We can't stay here long so get your personal belongings only. I'm going to go stand out front by the road and make sure he doesn't come back."

Amanda and I grabbed trash bags and she began packing her stuff from her room. I walked to my closet and was rather shocked to see his clothes spread out on both sides. Looking around, I found all of my clothing already in trash bags. I quickly got over my surprise and was truly grateful for the amount of time that had been saved by bagging up my stuff.

Walking through the house I saw evidence of his sisters everywhere. I felt an odd sense of violation that contradicted my relief at being out of the house. His sisters had been through all of my things. They had already decided what I could keep from my former life. The betrayal felt like a knife to my already wounded heart. There was nothing sacred. Nothing left untouched. I felt violated and emotionally raped.

The gun cabinet was no longer locked. The

tape recorder, once hidden in the drawer to record my phone conversations, was gone. The line under the carpet connecting it to the phone was no longer there. The sock in the baggie, no longer lying on the dresser. It was a normal bedroom, in a normal house. How could the terror of our last night together be wiped away as if nothing had ever happened? What a twisted fate. A household of lies.

I went through the house trying in my rushed state to remember other things that I might need. We started hauling our things out to the van. I had a brief moment of breakdown when our cat came in the house. I picked up the stray tiger cat we had adopted and I hugged him tight and cried. My heart broke because we couldn't take him with us and we had no idea what would become of him. We were both heartbroken to have leave him behind.

In her room Amanda was trying to decide what she could take and what she couldn't. How fair were rules that said we were only allowed to take our clothes and personal items? When marriages break, the unseen wounds often lie in the ones who have no voice. The little ones who suffer in silence without anyone listening to the cries of their hearts. Her guitar, her prized possession, was the only thing in her room that her heart cried out for.

I followed the trooper out the front door.

"Please, let her take it?"

"I can't give you that permission. Legally you can only take your personal items."

"That IS her personal item. She got it for Christmas."

"Mary, I'm going to walk out to the road to make sure he doesn't pull up. We need to wrap this up and get out of here. We've been here too long already." I watched him as he walked to the road and turned his back toward the house.

I raced back inside and wrapped her guitar in a blanket. Then I hurried out the door with it to the van. The guitar was nestled in its place in the van just in time as a familiar car flew into the driveway. Our trusted neighbor was true to his friendship and notified them we were there.

My sister-in-law did her best to try and convince Jan and the trooper she was there to show us love and support, a seemingly innocent act of family. Their actions were another reminder that I was not family. I was not the accepted one. I understood. I forgave them. Their allegiance was firmly in place.

My mother-in-law grabbed hold of me and pulled me tight. For all who were watching it might have seemed a tender moment, but the words whispered in my ear were anything but supportive.

"You need to stop this right now," she whispered.

I tried to pull away and she wouldn't let go.

"Stop this now," she commanded.

I pulled away and didn't respond. It was over. I would never be a part of the façade again. In that moment, I knew that I would never wear the mask again. The fear inside me turned to stone. The last flicker of hope that I would gain her acceptance and love was dead. Somehow, I would figure it out on my own without them. In my heart, I understood her pain, her torment, her heart. If I were put in the same position what would I do? I couldn't say.

Luckily, we had already gotten our things from the house, so the encounter didn't drag on. Amanda and I quickly got in the van and pulled out of the driveway one final time. Trooper Ernstes stayed behind speaking to them so he could make sure we weren't followed. I was grateful. As we drove away, I never looked back.

A few of those tiny, invisible cords were broken that day. The option of returning was removed from my grasp. That childish dream of being loved and accepted by his family was gone. The evil master, with his schemes of destruction was almost, but not quite, successful in completing his task of destroying my life. However, the master of abuse had underestimated his adversary, the One that shines light in dark places. For somewhere hidden in the darkest recesses of my heart, a tiny flicker of hope was fighting for someone to fan its flame.

## Chapter 5

The strength of those invisible cords that tie us together (as lovers, family, and friends) intricately unfolds throughout life in either love or pain. The intertwining of lives, hearts and souls, creates within, a beautiful flow and mingling of hearts when it is love that flows through those ties. However, when betrayal sets in motion a tide of hate, anger and rage, every life bound by that cord also feels the vengeful pull of the puppet master's spiteful hand.

The daytime hours were filled with tasks: court, finding permanent work, sending out resumes, trying to stretch the little bit of money we had, recovering from my back injury—my mind could barely contain all of the things I needed to do. I struggled to focus on all that lay before me. At times, I was sure my mind could not handle the pressure. Always near a breaking point, it was simply love for my daughter that saw me through. If it weren't for her, I would have given up.

Days were barely tolerable but as the shadows of night fell a dread flooded my soul that could not be contained. The ragged pain in my heart flooded my eyes. Choking back sobs, many nights were spent with my head buried in the pillow so Amanda would not hear my cries. Many a night, I slipped down the stairs under the cover of darkness and curled up in a chair in the living room and simply let the tears flow until I couldn't cry anymore.

What was this hold he had over me? Why did my heart cry out for a man who clearly didn't love me? Years I spent in humiliation at his endless infidelity and yet... my heart ached for the bond to be mended and made whole. No one understood my tears or the way my heart bled for him. I had no explanation for the way my body missed sleeping next to his at night. My mind screamed that I was insane and my heart cried out, "But I love him." How was it possible to have a deeply rooted love and hate for the same person? It didn't make sense. Perhaps I was crazy. Perhaps the taunts were true. How could I possibly ever be normal again? What was normal anyway? Did anyone really know?

Endless, merciless taunts flooded my heart

each night as the sun went down, *No one will ever love you… you will spend the rest of your life all alone… worthless… whore… loser….* The words never stopped running through my heart and mind. My bruises had healed. By all outward appearances there was no more evidence of a life of violence, but my heart was seared forever with words that cut deep and wounded, sacred places that only the giver of life would be able to reach and heal.

Every day I felt the pressure of shelter life. We were allowed thirty days and that was it. That incessant clock was ticking in my head, counting down the seconds until we would have to leave. Thankfully, the shelter had an aftercare transitional housing program. What an amazing hope at the end of this treacherous road. There would be assistance getting my own place. I barely dared to hope that it would be possible. Scouring the newspaper every day, I sought work like a madwoman. The rule for the program was you had to have a job, any job. The pressure was on. My fear was that I wouldn't be able to find a job and then I wouldn't qualify for the program. My back had still not healed. I still struggled to function in daily tasks. I had no idea how I would be able to work a full time job and handle all of the obstacles ahead of me. So many decisions to make, so little time for it all to work out. I tried not to complain but it was hard to keep up the painful pace every day. Amanda tried her best to cover my share of the household chores at the shelter.

The national economy was not helping me in any way. My new community was reeling from massive industry closings and hundreds of very skilled people were suddenly flooding the community looking for work. This made the search even harder for someone who had not worked in five years. My anxiety level rising, I feared I would miss my opportunity for help. One more thing that I couldn't do right. The whisper of ugly words kept repeating and rolling through my mind in waves. I couldn't escape the ebb and flow of taunts.

The days at the shelter passed quickly. Too quickly. Tick… Tock… tick… tock. *You're almost out of time! Then what are you going to do? You're going to lose her you know.* The ugly, sinister voice just wouldn't stop taunting me. The shelter had become our refuge. Our safe place. It felt good there. We never wanted to leave.

The shelter became a place where Amanda could finally be herself. She quickly became a favorite of the staff at both the shelter and the crisis center. Her fragile and ultra-polite demeanor won the hearts of all who spent time with her. Her complete and utter brokenness brought even the toughest of social workers to tears. We were so touched every day by the volunteers, interns and staff. They went the extra mile for us. Interns would ask Amanda to ride with them as they transported other residents to appointments, they would both come back with Starbucks and they kept the pantry shelves stocked with foods she liked to eat. Another time, the program director just happened to have passes for the movie Amanda badly wanted to see. Those little things meant so very much.

Life in a shelter is very surreal. The outside world continues on its daily routine while every moment in a shelter is a gigantic struggle just for human existence. Starting over from nothing brings out one's primal instincts of survival. I quickly realized the things in life I had always taken for granted: a roof over my head, clothing, food, hygiene products, dishes to eat from, spices, silverware, hot showers, towels, clean sheets. Each little item left behind in the haste to flee, became another reminder of great sadness and loss. Not to mention family photos and heirlooms, treasured gifts from years gone by, the keepsakes from childbirth—all are painful reminders that it can be lost in a moment, irreplaceable.

Mother's Day was special.

Amanda was so happy. I walked into the

kitchen at the shelter to find a cake she had baked just for me. I smiled and tried to hold back my tears.

"I got a gift for you."

She handed me her wonderful Mother's Day offering.

I set the wrapped gift on the counter so I could open her card. The outside of the card was a colored pencil drawing of flowers hand drawn by Amanda. I recognized the amount of time and attention it took for her to create that masterpiece for me.

Next was the gift I wasn't expecting. I wasn't sure where she got the money or how she pulled it off but I was sure her accomplice was somewhere in the house. Jesse, the intern, had become an ally who helped Amanda along the way.

A new purse was just what a girl needs to make her day brighter. I was happy. Gifts didn't matter in the grander scheme of things. We were together. We were safe. We were healing.

There is great, world-changing, power in simple acts of kindness. The master of evil and darkness uses tactics of hate to destroy, but for all of his schemes his work is left as rubble in the light of simple acts of kindness given without motive or scheme. Unconditional grace usurps the power of hatred.

The school year was nearly over and I hated to ask Amanda to start a new school, from a shelter, at the end of the year.

"She can catch the bus right here from the shelter," Jan told me.

"I understand that but what's going to protect her at school if he shows up and tries to take her?"

"Really, without a court order, there's nothing to stop him from checking her out and taking her. She's only protected under the protective order when she is with you because he can't come near you. Protective orders in Michigan don't include children. You must have a court order to keep him from her."

I wasn't willing to risk it. I didn't know what my options were but I was willing to try anything. I gave the school counselor a call at her school in Allegan and shared everything that was going on.

"Mrs. Clemons, your husband has been to the school every day looking for Amanda. I figured something was going on. Do you have any paperwork from the court to validate what you're telling me? Just so we can have something documented?"

"I have a protective order."

"That will work. I will get with all of her teachers and let them know what's going on. If you give me a couple of days, you can come to the office and pick up assignments."

"I'm really scared to come there and run the risk of him showing up."

"Maybe we can work something out so Amanda can communicate with her teachers by email and then you would only have to come every couple of weeks to drop off her completed work."

"Thank you, for working with us. We can do that." I sighed with relief as I hung up the phone.

What a blessing it was to find that others surrounded us with love and support. Our hearts cried out in relief. The shelter manager helped her create an email address so she could receive assignments from her teachers. Every couple of weeks, I made the dangerous trek back to her school for an assignment exchange.

So many decisions had to be made. It was difficult to process all that I was learning about myself, about him, about the system: protective orders, divorce, criminal charges, and custody. It was all just too much to take in. In my heart I just wanted it all to go away. All the years of praying for what was broken to be fixed seemed to be for naught. I stayed for years hoping for change. Now that dream mocked me in the day and tormented me at night.

*You weren't good enough. You failed. You didn't have enough faith.*

"I couldn't change myself enough to fix it. I tried. I really did. God, please, forgive me. I didn't mean to fail you."

Those were the cries of my broken heart in the darkness of night when no one was around. I felt forsaken and alone in a house full of people. Broken. As I lay in the darkness of night, somehow a realization began to dawn in the recesses of my soul. It wasn't my calling in life to "fix" him. Martyrdom wasn't my purpose. My existence was not for the purpose of laying down my life for a man. From somewhere beyond the darkest abyss, those acts of kindness coupled with healing words, began to bring light into the dark places. "*You* are worthy! *You* are already loved, my precious baby girl."

We settled into the routine of shelter life: support group, classes, chores, homework, looking for work. I went through the motions of each and every day but there was something missing that was as necessary as breathing: church. My heart cried out to not be forsaken by God. I was afraid I had gone too far by leaving. Divorce carried eternal consequences. I teetered on the edge of despair. Words spoken into my spirit by others said if I divorced, I could never remarry or I would burn in hell. How could this be? Was I to remain single and alone for the rest of my days? Was this just one more punishment for not being able to wear the mask well enough or continue playing the game? It didn't make sense. So many rules in serving God. So easily damned to hell--or so I had been told.

The doctrine of our church taught that we were separate from the world and that our way of believing brought "truth" that others didn't possess. In this strict, legalistic doctrine I was taught that I couldn't trust the words and intent of people who didn't share our faith. I heard the words of the advocates around me, but my heart rejected their theology because I needed to hear it from someone in my faith. Oh how the master deceiver was at work in my life. Whispered words in my ear, I could not discern truth from lies. The Bible, which had been my compass, was compromised by my brokenness and by the sinister taunts from that ever present shadowy presence of death.

The battle raged on inside of my spirit and soul. I struggled daily with the battle between beliefs of our church and my own personal fight for life. At a crossroads of eternal salvation, I had to make some decisions, decisions that could cost me eternally. At the age of 13, I had pledged my life to God. With every fiber of my being, I desired to serve Him and do as He asked, even if it meant it would cost me my life. Religion taught death was a small price to pay for eternity. Religion had taught me that a good wife stays, a good wife submits--which in my case meant, a good wife ultimately died. My soul cried out for this not to be my fate. I desperately wanted to live. I fought a silent, secret desire inside my spirit to also be loved. I desperately needed to be loved. Through grace I was shown that not all preachers shared the same beliefs about divorce as my in-laws had taught. After several hours on the phone visiting with my brother's pastor, who shared with me much about covenant vows, I could not shake the guilt I felt at the thought of filing for divorce, even though I knew I had no choice. Guilt and grace continued their battle for my eternal soul. Finally, grace trumped guilt and for me, there was no turning back.

The legal aid office was an intimidating place. I had no idea what I was doing or what I was asking for. The attorney assigned to my case was very lawyer-like in appearance and very non-descript in attire. His highly professional demeanor calmed my nerves but also left me skeptical as to his devotion to actually helping me with my case.

I had to establish residency in my new community before I could file divorce papers there. I didn't want to wait. I needed to do it quickly so I couldn't change my mind. I needed to commit to that life-changing step, but I had to wait.

With each new obstacle I faced, my anger mounted. I was the victim. He was the criminal. How was any of this horrible nightmare fair? I was the one paying the price. His own flesh and blood child and I were homeless because of his decisions to batter. I was injured because of his decision to hurt me. I was humiliated and left starting over while he continued to live in MY grandparent's former home. He was the hunter and we were his prey. Nothing about this journey was fair.

Somehow, it felt as if all of the consequences of his decision to batter fell solely upon me and my child. My heart could not fathom a gracious or loving God who could punish a child simply for seeking freedom from death's harrowing grip.

Every day a spiritual battle raged within me... truth and lies... scriptures engrained on my heart... words condemning and judging with every breath I took. More than anything I wanted to be accepted and loved by the Father but the hissing voice in my ear only reaffirmed my damnation. I was at a crossroads of belief: do I continue to believe in this fearsome God I couldn't see who demanded absolutes and extended little mercy, or did I walk away from a church that wasn't loving or supportive and hadn't extended any grace?

I felt suspended in a world in which I didn't fit. My plain, unadorned face and clothing, uncut hair and long skirts caused me to stand out in a world that I wasn't familiar with. Isolation had become my friend. I was overweight and out of shape. The years of not having a job—sheltered—had kept me from the things of this world and the people in it. As I struggled to adjust, I was forced to look deep within myself and seek out truth. The lines were blurred and heaven was silent. My heart felt forsaken by all who were supposed to care. Never before had I felt so alone.

Getting ready for a job interview, I studied my reflection in the mirror and I hated the reflection I saw. Plain simple face, bushy eyebrows, honey blonde hair that seemed to go on forever, innocent, sheltered from the world. My heart broke for the woman who was reflected before me. She had to face a cold, uncaring world and try to find her way. I wasn't sure I could do it but I knew I had no choice. If I could not do it for myself, I HAD to do it for the child who was depending solely on me for her survival. Squaring my shoulders back, I headed out the door to spend some of the precious few dollars I possessed to purchase some makeup from a discount store.

As the end of our thirty-day stay began to

draw near, I started to panic as I still hadn't been able to find a job. I was getting desperate. It was harder than I ever thought possible. I finally gave in and applied for a job with a temp agency, willing to take anything. I had run out of options. We needed to be accepted into the transitional housing program. I wasn't prepared for all of the testing the agency required of each applicant. One more hurdle to overcome. I was determined to do the best I could. I would NOT be defeated.

After a few agonizing days of waiting, the temp agency finally called. They had a position for me: working night shift in an automobile factory. THAT was definitely NOT what I was expecting. A cushy office job, perhaps, but factory work was not for me. Somehow I managed to suppress the urge to immediately turn down the offer, which was a good thing because they had nothing else to offer me.

The thought of it scared me to death. I had never worked nights and I had never worked in a factory. The thought of working on a production line terrified me. I was scared I wouldn't be able to hold up under the pressure of being timed for production.

A lot of companies in the auto industry hire their workers as temporary employees to begin with and then offer them permanent positions after a period of time. It was better than nothing but I dreaded it with every single ounce of my being.

My first night of work I was nearly sick to my stomach. Amanda was safe and snug in her bed at the shelter. I didn't have to worry about her. Walking outside in the darkness of night was terrifying. What if he was out there somewhere? Waiting? The fear of the darkness almost kept me from taking the job. However, fear of a future without a home and without my daughter was enough to force me out that door.

As I drove into the parking lot at 10:30 at night, I seriously considered turning right back around and heading back to the shelter. I couldn't believe I was actually going to do it. My heart racing in my chest, I forged ahead and found a parking space. Choking back fear, I marched myself up to the door of the massive warehouse-style building.

I was pleasantly surprised when I walked inside. Just beyond a large foyer was an open break area with a snack bar. Just beyond the break area were the different assembly lines. It was bright and cheerful. I was expecting a dark, dismal environment in an old warehouse. I wasn't expecting a new, modern facility. However, it was still intimidating for someone who had never stepped foot in a factory.

That was the first night of the longest two

weeks of my life. I found myself installing dashes, radios and wiring harnesses for Ford Windstar vans. I wasn't good at it. I feared that some unsuspecting soul would purchase their brand new van and would quickly learn that absolutely nothing in their dash worked. Thank goodness for quality control inspectors. I spent every second of the night worrying that I was going to be the cause of a major back up on the assembly line and the rest of the line workers would hunt me down for costing them their jobs.

At 7:00 each morning, I drove home exhausted. Making the adjustment to working nights was challenging. The fact I was a single mom didn't change one bit just because I was working nights. It also didn't take away all of the other stuff I had to accomplish during the day. Sleeping in a shelter during the day is a challenge all in itself. It was incredibly difficult trying to continue looking for permanent work, comply with all of the shelter requirements, heal from my back injury, deal with the police investigation and the court stuff and begin looking for an apartment.

Not a single day went by that I wasn't stressed and emotionally exhausted. Physically, my body could barely keep up the pace. But there was no one else to do it for me. There was not a

Plan B. There was not an opt-out plan. I was it. By day, I continued to submit resumes and move forward on our journey to freedom. I dreaded the nights, but I would put on my happy mask and trudge my way to the factory.

After a few days, during my daily ritual of scouring through the classifieds, I ran across an ad for an Office Manager. Excitement began to bubble up in my spirit. During my last five years of being confined to the house, I had taught myself to type, to create business letters and documents and studied office etiquette.

It didn't say what kind of business it was, but I knew I could do all of the duties listed in the ad. I faxed my resume as requested then waited. Miraculously, I received a call to schedule an interview. It was a miracle, or (more likely) it was my shadow guardian named Grace.

My banking experience as a teller had been the extent of my office experience. I had retail down to a science but was still a little rough at administrative work, however, determined I could learn it all. We scheduled a time to meet and I was so excited. I couldn't wait.

As I parked my car in front of the address I was given, my nerves and self-doubt almost got the better of me. Nationwide Insurance. I would never have thought in a million years that it would even be possible to hold such a position.

It was nothing he would have ever allowed me to do.

Cindy, the agency owner, was rather intimidating but was quite nice overall. Her gruff demeanor was rather off-putting, but she seemed to like me. As I left, I was hopeful that I might actually have a chance at the position.

The next day Martha, a shelter volunteer was driving me back from class and while we were talking the subject of my interview came up.

"Where was your interview?" She asked me in her kind manner. She was also a survivor. She understood me in ways the other workers didn't.

"Nationwide."

"WHAT? Are you serious? With Cindy?"

I looked at her in amazement. "You know her?"

"My husband actually owns the business right next door to her."

I started to get excited. Perhaps I was about to get a break. Grace was working overtime on my behalf.

"Watch this!" She pulled out her cell phone and dialed a number.

"Hey would you walk over to Nationwide and tell Cindy I need to talk to her…."

I listened in amazement as this person whom I barely knew, this sister of experience, was vouching for me—a stranger—for a job I wasn't even sure I was qualified for. The first spark of a hope for a future burst to life within me and I couldn't hold back the momentary giggle of happiness.

## Chapter 6

Days and nights started to blur together as I struggled to adjust to working night shifts but the days were flying by. The end of my thirty day shelter stay was drawing near. The shelter staff began preparing to move back into the main shelter and give up the lease on the rented house, so those of us living there were extended a few extra days as they didn't want to take anyone new into the house.

After about two weeks of working at the factory, Cindy from Nationwide called me back. Her idea of a second interview was rather creative but also very effective.

"A big part of our business is telemarketing. My office manager needs to be able to train and manage the telemarketers along with the office staff. The only way you can train them is if you know how to do it yourself. I'd like you to come in and work a couple of evenings as a telemarketer and see if it's something that you would even be interested in doing."

Telemarketing was not something I had ever done before but I did have a lot of customer service training from the banking industry. How hard could it be?

"I'll try it."

"Great."

After three hours of being hung up on, leaving messages and stumbling through the script, I began to wonder which was worse: factory work or telemarketing. I despised them both. I was horrible at reading the script. I had conflict issues to begin with and people are just *rude* to telemarketers.

"I'll let you know in a few days what I decide."

I went back to the factory and continued the drudgery. Some people thrive and actually enjoy the continuity of factory work and I admire them. Other people are personable and incredibly good at telephone sales. Those people amaze me. I was neither. It only took me a few nights on an assembly line to discover that I get bored easily. My mind wandered. I needed to multitask. I needed a job that challenged me and forced me to stretch my limits. Telemarketing and factory work were not for me.

I impatiently waited to hear back from Cindy

at Nationwide and was completely ecstatic when the call finally came. I couldn't believe it. I agreed to start the following week. Things were finally starting to turn around.

Then my mom decided to relocate to Georgia. I was in shock. It was totally unexpected. She was my support system. She was also my go between for contact with my husband. She made arrangements to pick up more of our clothes and items from the house. She kept him appeased so he would leave us somewhat alone. I felt sick at the thought that I might actually have to speak to him myself. Every time we separated in the past and I gave in and spoke to him—*I went back*. I didn't trust myself to be strong if I had to have communication with him directly. He knew exactly how to break down my defenses. I couldn't give him that opportunity again.

My heart hurt and I felt betrayed by her decision to move. I felt like it was just one more person to walk out on me. It added one more layer to the wall I was building in my heart. People walking away from me wasn't anything new. I would be okay. I always was. More of those destructive voices were speaking lies into my spirit.

Mom didn't waste any time in planning her move. In less a month from returning from Atlanta, she was packed up and gone. Part of me understood. It wasn't easy dealing with his family. They were brutal. They spent their time stalking and harassing my family. Part of me wished we could have gone with her.

While a world full of people continued their lives around me, I continued to build that silent wall around the broken pieces of my heart. My only defense was to keep up the pretense that all was well inside of me. No longer could I risk allowing people inside the wall. The risk was too great. Although I loved others deeply, it seemed as if I was incapable of trusting anyone. Amanda was the only exception and sometimes it was hard to bridge the gap between us as well. Power and Control are foes worthy of great note. Once they begin their assault on the heart, many are powerless to fight back. I feared that never again would the pieces of my innermost being ever fit together again. For all the world to see, I was a success story. I was making it. I was overcoming, but on the inside a battle was raging. Those shadowing voices kept up with the onslaught of doubt and fear.

I applied and we were approved for the transitional housing program. However, we were required to find our own place and obtain our own lease. I didn't have a dime for a down payment and I wasn't sure just what I would have in the way of furniture but it didn't matter.

We would have our very own place where we were safe.

Amanda and I frantically searched for an apartment. Unfamiliar with our new community, we searched high and low. Pulling up to a townhome in a residential area we were excited. It had a garage, two bedrooms and basically would meet all of our needs, although I had a few safety concerns about the home and it was kind of small. It moved to the top of the list, but we decided to look at a few more options.

Then we found the perfect location. The area was nice and it was only about three blocks from the Nationwide Agency. We first looked at a bottom floor apartment but we just didn't feel comfortable with it. The ceilings were low. The apartment was dark and gloomy and it just didn't feel inviting. It felt like a cave. The apartment also came with a sliding glass door and patio. As it was on the ground floor this, in itself, was enough to send me running from the building. The thought of him being able to have that ease of access to us was more than my heart could take. Even though the exterior entrance to the building was locked, the sliding glass door was a deal-breaker.

"I have another unit available on the third floor if you'd like to look at it?" The manager was very sweet. "It is basically the same floor plan but it has vaulted ceilings and has a very open feel."

We made the trek up three flights of stairs. We knew it was the one as soon as we walked in the door. Vaulted ceilings made it feel twice as big as it really was. It had a living room, dining area and kitchen in that big open space. It felt so grand and it was going to be all ours. The living room opened up onto our own balcony. I was comforted in the thought that someone would have to climb up and over the balcony below us in order to reach ours. I felt safe. We had two bedrooms and two full bathrooms. It was clean and well-maintained. We could look out the window and see our assigned parking space below. Our carport space was the very first space, next to the sidewalk that led to the front entrance. It was perfect. It had enough safety precautions that I didn't think I would be able to find all of that together at any other location.

Another positive was that several other ladies in the building were also part of the transitional housing program. It was like our very own support group, right there in the building. I was on cloud nine at all of the good things beginning to happen. Finally, there was some light at the end of the tunnel.

The rent was affordable but I didn't know where I was going to come up with deposit money.

I met with my case manager and she referred me to another program in the community that often gave rent assistance. I later realized that she had known all along that it was going to be just fine for me, but she was making me do as much for myself as I could. Their role at the agency was to fill in the gaps. I am so thankful.

*****

All was eerily silent from the enemy camp during this time. *The silence before the storm*. There were actually days when I wasn't completely blinded by fear. My heart began to hope that he was finally going to leave me alone. I prayed the protective order would serve its purpose and he would just let things go and move on.

The puppet master is sneaky in his attempts to manipulate. All the characters have specific roles to play, and he is strict in his mastery that all should comply and stick with the script. As it always is for the hunter and its prey, a vicious game of suspense as the hunter lurks in the shadows waiting for his unsuspecting prey to let down its guard for just a moment. Such as it is in this fight for power, the hunter tries to lure the prey with flattery and promises only to grow angry if this ploy no longer works. Both the hunter and prey are but simple pawns in this vicious pattern of life. The eerie echo of laughter, not heard by human ears, but felt with a dark chill that penetrates the spirits of both as the bitter play continues to unfold resounds.

*****

There was so much to do. I didn't have a single dime to pay for all of the things we needed. It was overwhelming. My mom left most of her furniture and household items for me in my brother's garage. I had no idea what was there, but it was comforting to have familiar things to surround us. All of our stuff was beyond our reach.

I tried to move forward and think positive thoughts, but there were times that grief would overtake my spirit. I would weep over the little things we had lost: family photos, Manda's baby pictures, gifts from family and things given to me by my deceased grandparents. My grandmother's cookbook, my old upright piano, Amanda's doll collection, her toys… our things. Our life. I knew it was all just "stuff," but it was *OUR* stuff. It represented our past and family and events that mattered. Oh, the endless sadness and countless tears that are shed when memories are wrapped up in inanimate things. The pain of letting go was just another loss, another tear in the heart that no longer trusted.

I jumped through every hoop necessary and completed the paperwork, applied, and was approved for funding the deposit. My case manager gave me a voucher for a sofa from a second-hand store. I begged for assistance to move us into the apartment. Then the moving process began. It was nothing short of a hard-earned miracle, but we had our keys.

Conflicting emotions struck us both as we packed up our room in the shelter. Amanda felt a loss of her newfound sense of security, friendship and freedom. I struggle with feelings of my loss of a safety net. The shelter shrouded us in a cocoon of sorts. It kept us safe from predators and harm while we struggled through the process of transformation from victims to survivors. With each packed bag, we broke free of the cocoon more and more. We were excited to start our new adventure, but there was still something terrifying about leaving the first safe place we had ever experienced.

Amanda and I toted bag after bag containing our clothing and personal items down the stairs and to our car. Then at the apartment, the cycle was reversed: out of the car, up the stairs and into the apartment. I wasn't sure what we were going to do in the way of beds but we didn't care if we had to sleep on the floor. It just didn't matter. We were home.

The crisis center loaned me enough money to rent a U-Haul truck to move the furniture and household items my mom left for me with my brother. This meant we had to make yet another trip back to our home town. We were both nervous and excited. I had no idea what would be in the boxes waiting for us. I didn't care. Anything was more than we had.

Cautiously we made our way back to familiar territory. We were totally conscious of the fact that my husband had assigned each of his siblings to the task of following each member of my family in his attempt to locate us. Every fiber of my being was aware that we may very well be leading them straight to our new home but I didn't know any other way for us to get the things we needed. The move had to be done, and I couldn't expect my brother and his wife to do it all for me.

We arrived at my brother's house and I was glad to see my nephews and just enjoy the feeling of normalcy that comes from being with family. There was so much I didn't know about my own family. A myriad of thoughts raced through my mind ranging from happiness, to sadness and regret. I had missed out on so much of their lives.

They led me to the garage and showed me all that Mom had left for us. It felt like Christmas. We now had a dining room set, a queen size bed, décor items, dishes and a mixture of other household items. I was so grateful. It didn't change the fact that I owned my own home which was still full of my things, only a few miles away, but it helped. It helped, a lot.

We loaded all of it into the U-Haul and prepared to take it to my house. I wasn't able to do very much lifting due to my back injury but I helped as much as I could. I watched the road, in all directions, waiting for the house to become surrounded by my in-laws. As soon as the truck was loaded, we made our way back to Holland, to our new life.

Over the next few days we unpacked and settled in. We put away the dishes and decorated the walls without fear of angry reprisal. The shelter staff also allowed us to pick out items from their little store room. My favorite gift from them was a clothes basket full of cleaning products, paper products, a mop and a broom. With every item gifted to us, we had more than enough to live comfortably. It was our own. It was comfortable. My mom's items surrounding us brought us great comfort. Many of her things even smelled like her home and we felt safe. It gave us a sense of normalcy.

I struggled with anxiety and fear. Every day. I was provided with a cell phone from the shelter that only had 911 capability. I held it close and never left the apartment without it. I carried it with me to take out the trash and I carried it with me to the laundry room at the back of the building. As I pushed myself forward and tried to break the strong-holds of my past, I fought past the triggers that constantly plagued me.

I would walk through Walmart without a time limit that was liberating and terrifying at the same time. After being in the store for a while, it felt as if my body could sense time was about to run out. A sick sense would rise from the pit of my stomach telling me I had to leave. The more I ignored the rising sense of panic, the worse it got until I had to flee the store and go home. Home was safe. I realized very quickly that I needed to find a way to control the feelings of panic that arose in those moments. It didn't matter if I was at church, at work, at home, it didn't matter. After fourteen years of living on a strict schedule, it was hard to break the habit.

The job at Nationwide was a million times harder than I had expected. I didn't realize that I would need a license from the state to do my job and I was terrified of the process of obtaining it. My boss's idea of "training" was to show me how to do *one* auto quote, *one* renter's quote, *one* homeowner's quote, and then how to convert the quote into a policy. After that, she would point to a huge manual and tell me "to look it up." I also had to learn how to do all of the customer paperwork, payments, changes, marketing, cold calling, filing, underwriting, home inspections, plus supervise telemarketers. It was almost more than my traumatized mind could absorb, in addition to everything else. Every day was a massive overload of responsibility and information.

At the same time was an on-going criminal investigation of my husband, our divorce case, and studying for my Property & Casualty license. I was desperate to make it work or I would have been forced to go back to the factory job. My stress level was through the roof. Financially we were okay but I had never had a position like this before.

A few weeks after moving into our apartment, the State Trooper called me at home. We had kept in regular contact and talked at least once a week. Everyone warned me not to get my hopes up about criminal charges against my husband because he had no prior convictions. I had no expectations there would be any kind of charges brought against him.

"I just wanted to let you know that I got a warrant back from the DA's office."

I was not prepared to hear that. Part of me wanted him to go to jail for a long time. I wanted him to pay and I wanted some vindication for all that he had put me through. Part of me was terrified of what he would do to me if he got the chance.

So many emotions raced through my mind. Guilt reared its ugly head and I struggled to hold it back. If I had just kept my mouth shut. If I had remained silent, he wouldn't be looking at jail time. However, I was the victim, and he was the criminal. It felt like heaven and hell were at war around me and the clanking of swords told of the battle for my soul. I should have been a better wife... but God knows how hard I tried… back and forth the battle raged.

Guilt is often a sneaky lie. Its weight was almost more than I could bear as it whispered its lies into my ear and heart. Its partner, Shame, also lurks in darkness as it works to wrap its victim in a shroud of despair. These companion cords continued to control me and threatened to force me to retreat from the light.

"I really wasn't expecting this, but the DA issued a warrant for Aggravated Assault with Attempt to Commit Murder."

Surely I misunderstood. It was too much. I couldn't believe it. I was happy and scared at the same time. I was happy that people with authority had really "heard" me and more importantly, they believed me. I was scared of repercussions from my husband and his family.

"I'm going to be off for the next few days but as soon as I'm back on duty, we are going to try to pick him up. We went by your house already but we haven't been able to catch him there. We don't really want to pick him up at work, but we will if we have to."

"Thank you for the warning." I was terrified of what would happen when they tried to arrest him. I just knew he would try something crazy. It would be even worse if they arrested him at work.

"I'll keep you posted and I'll let you know when we pick him up."

"Thank you."

Trying to choke down the nausea, I had to tell Amanda that her daddy was going to be arrested. We lived the next few days in both a total sense of fear and anticipation of freedom. I waited by the phone for word that he was in jail. We worked on settling into the apartment and I continued my training at the office. I also changed my address on my driver's license.

A few nights later, the sound of our door buzzer woke me from a sound sleep. Whoever was trying to get into the building was persistent. Cautiously, without turning on any lights I made my way to the bedroom window, the shadows of darkness covering me in security. With a shaking hand, I peeked out through the blinds and tried to see the sidewalk at the front of the building. Barely, I made the shapes of two shadowy figures in the darkness. They moved away from the door and the light above the entrance cast an eerie glow around them. I recognized them immediately. Two of his sisters were knocking and ringing the bell. Instantly, I immediately knew the reason why. He had been arrested.

I had to know for sure. Fumbling through all my paperwork, I found the number for the county jail in the area where we were from. I needed to know but part of me didn't want to. I just wanted it all to go away, a bad dream, a nightmare that I would wake up from. My entire body shook from fear. I wasn't sure I would be able to hold a conversation on the phone. Even my teeth were chattering.

"I just wanted to check…"

"Yes, ma'am, they brought him in just a little while ago."

"I knew you had because his sisters are downstairs right now trying to get into my apartment building."

"Ma'am, you need to call the sheriff's department and report it."

"Thank you, I will."

Cautiously, I made my way down the hallway. My entire being was wracked with fear that they would somehow get the deadbolt, the door lock and the chain undone to gain access to our apartment. Amanda came out of her room to see what was going on.

"Who is it?" she asked in a voice groggy from sleep.

"They found us."

"How did they find us?"

"I don't know. But they are outside right now."

I watched from the window while we waited for the police. Eventually they gave up and walked away.

Two sheriff's deputies came into our apartment a little while later.

"Ma'am, it isn't a crime for them to enter this building."

"Isn't this private property? I don't want them here. I have a protective order against their brother. The downstairs door is locked. I don't think you understand how bad our case is."

"Ma'am people come and go all the time in apartment buildings. There's really nothing we can do."

"Really?" I was devastated. How was I supposed to protect us if the police refused to do anything? The officers left without taking a report.

At least I could rest assured that he was in jail, but I knew that it wouldn't last long. No matter what they had to do and no matter how high the bond, they would post it. He wouldn't let them rest until they did. We didn't get much sleep the rest of the night.

In the morning, I started calling and leaving messages for Trooper Ernstes. My phone rang about the time he normally went on duty.

"Mary, I'm sorry. I wanted to be the one to pick him up but he got picked up on a routine traffic stop while I was off."

"So what happens now?" I didn't want to go to court. I didn't want to face him in court. I would give anything in the world to not have to do that. EVER. I wished that someone could just wave a magic wand and transport us to another time and place where I would never have to deal with him again. I just wanted it all to stop, and yet the war waged on. I felt sick to my stomach.

"There will be a hearing. You will have to testify and tell the judge what happened."

"My husband's sisters showed up at my apartment and when I called the police they wouldn't even take a report."

"Did you happen to get their names?"

"Yes, sir."

It was a nightmare that just wouldn't end.

WHY? WHY? WHY? Did he have to call the police? I would never have reported him to the police but he had to report me? REALLY? That I was abusive. REALLY? My mind was reeling from it all. Why couldn't he just let us go? Why did it have to come to this? Didn't he understand I wasn't trying to hurt him? I wasn't going to try to get him in trouble. I just wanted him to stop hurting me. I just wanted it all to stop. He was my heart. I had committed my whole heart to him and this is how it was going to end? My mind struggled to grasp the implications of all that had transpired. The puppet master continued his frightful saga as he drew the actors back onto the stage to perform their painful dance to entertain the evil watchers.

Later in the day, the same two deputies from a few nights before came back to the apartment to take a report. "Ms. Clemons, we would like to apologize. We didn't fully understand the extent of the situation until talking with Trooper Ernstes. We will place this address on our watch list so if you call 911 again, the officers will know."

I forced myself to be polite but it was so hard. I was angry. I was angry that during the first visit, I was just another woman calling to complain from an apartment complex. No one important. Just another complaint. A snarky satisfaction welled up inside of me as they apologized so profusely for the lack of understanding on their prior visit. I was deeply saddened that it took a call from another officer to get their attention.

Anger continued to whisper its venom into my ear. I couldn't contain it. I went from the heights of great hope to the depths of dismal despair. I never asked to be in this position. I just wanted to stop getting hurt. Why was that so wrong? Why was I the bad guy? It didn't make any sense. How could someone get away with this for so long AND have people stand and defend him? When did wrong become right and right become wrong? Little roots of bitterness began to take hold in my heart.

Fear ensured that I carried my 911 cell phone with me everywhere. I constantly checked it to make sure it was charged and working. A few weeks later, my cousin was staying with us and I was glad. Her company kept Amanda occupied while I was at work.

Early one morning, I told them goodbye and made my way down the stairs to my car. Out of habit, I locked the doors as soon as I was seated in the car. Before I even realized what had happened, a truck pulled up behind my car, blocking my escape. Startled, I looked up to see my brother-in-law and sister-in-law beating on the window of my car.

My sister-in-law yelled through the glass as

her hand slapped the window, "You know you're lying. You need to stop this! ARE YOU GOING TO TESTIFY? ARE YOU?"

She moved to the front of my car and got up on the front bumper and continued her tirade. My brother-in-law held his position next to the driver side door. He continued hitting the window and called me a liar over and over.

"9-1-1 what is your emergency?"

I was nearly frozen with fear and barely able to describe the scene to the dispatcher.

"My daughter and I just moved out of a shelter and my husband was arrested for attempted murder... His sister and her husband have me blocked in. I'm in in my car. She's beating on the hood of my car and he's hitting my window."

"Ok, ma'am, we have officers on the way." The yelling continued but he couldn't make out what they were saying. "What did she just say, ma'am?"

"She's yelling 'are you going to testify?'"

I kept repeating everything I could understand to the dispatcher.

Amanda and my cousin were watching what was happening from our living room window and were also on the phone with 911. Suddenly, they both bolted back to the truck he was driving. As they headed toward the exit I read the license plate to the dispatcher.

Shaken, I went back into the building while I waited for law enforcement to arrive. My heart wouldn't stop racing. Would I ever feel safe again? I just didn't know. Heart full of conflicting emotions, I just wanted it all to stop. I didn't want to spend the rest of my life dealing with their ugliness. I didn't want to fight anymore.

When the officers arrived I was disappointed once again.

"Ma'am the license number you gave us is registered to a man with a Holland address not your brother or sister-in-law."

"I repeated it to the dispatcher several times. I don't know why it isn't registered to them. It's not a vehicle I've ever seen before so I'm assuming it's a new vehicle they just bought."

"Ma'am, since we don't have any evidence of the incident, there really isn't anything we can do."

After the police left, my neighbor on the first floor stopped me in the hall.

"Hey, I heard about what happened this morning. I came in earlier this morning and I think I let your sister-in-law in the building. She was outside ringing the buzzer and I just let her in when I came in. Then I heard her upstairs knocking on your door. She knocked for a long while."

I stared at her in shock.

"I guess I slept through it. I took a valium last night because I couldn't sleep."

I couldn't believe she had actually gotten in the building. She had tried to get into my apartment. Would it ever end? Grateful for a lock in the handle, a deadbolt and a chain on my door, I knew we were safe inside our apartment. Anywhere else on the property... not so much.

Frustration at the whole wretched legal system shook me to my core. There was really no way to truly be safe if the police weren't even able to protect you when you needed them. I did everything I could afford or think of to provide a safe home for my daughter and my best just wasn't good enough.

Surely the puppet master was pleased with his work. The threads of Power and Control had an ever-reaching hand. He wielded his control through other unwitting participants who didn't even realize they were part of the dance. The players entered and exited the stage at the will and control of the master, mere entertainment for evil watchers.

Trooper Ernstes took that frightening event back to the prosecutor to seek Witness Tampering charges and the DA decided that if it happened again, they would seek charges, but for the moment they would just amend the protective order. Their thought was that amending the protective order to read "No direct or indirect contact (through family or friends)" would have a much bigger impact. If they contacted us again, he would go to jail.

The date of the first court hearing quickly approached. I couldn't believe I was actually going to have to do this. The last place I wanted to be in the entire world was in that court room. My case manager picked me up from my apartment and drove me to the courthouse. Trooper Ernstes met us in the parking lot and escorted us to the waiting area.

I was so scared. I had never testified in court before. The roiling of my stomach was almost my undoing. I didn't want to see him. Shame and guilt washed over me in waves. I didn't want to share all of our stuff to a room full of strangers who didn't know us or care about us. How did our lives get to this place where we were on display? Every word I spoke was open for attack. I felt condemnation, shame and judgment oozing from every corner of the room. I was overwhelmed by all of it. Shame whispered lies into my mind and tried to convince me not to talk.

*No one is going to believe you. Do you want everyone to know? They don't care about you.*

Then fear stepped in and added its two cents.

*He's going to kill you if you say anything. You know he will. You know what he said he'd do.*

Every threat replayed in my mind: I couldn't get the image of the possum hanging dead, in a tree at the side of our yard out of my head. He had shot it and left it hanging, entrails stringing down from the tree, as a reminder, to me—"If you leave me, I'll do the same thing to you and your brothers and your mom that I did to that possum in the tree."

I believed him.

The war waged on in my mind as I tried to sift through what questions I might be asked and what I would say in response. I wish I could just disappear and the whole thing would just go away.

Trooper Ernstes proved to be very entertaining in the waiting room. He worked hard to distract us. There was a TV mounted on the wall showing a sports program, and the room was full of other officers waiting to testify on other cases. The feeling was surreal. I was there in that room but part of me wasn't. I wanted it to be over so badly.

All too soon they called us into the courtroom. My advocate, Jan, found a seat in the packed courtroom. Trooper Ernstes took a seat at the table next to the prosecutor. I took my seat on the witness stand. I looked at my husband, sitting at the defendant's table. He looked like he had lost weight. His eyes were sad, but I also saw a glimpse of something only I knew to look for. It scared me. My heart broke at the sight of him. I didn't want to do this. He was good at the deception. I couldn't figure out what was real and what was part of the act for everyone else. My heart wanted to believe he had changed. My mind told me to wise up and move on.

"Would you please state your name for the record?"

"Mary Clemons."

"Do you swear to tell the truth, the whole truth, and nothing but the truth so help you God?"

"I do."

I prayed I wouldn't throw up right there in front of everybody. I could not wrap my mind around how we got to this place. Another part of me, the bitter part, said he deserved it. He caused this. He abused me. He called the police on me. Was I a perfect wife? NO. Did I make mistakes? YES. Did I deserve to be beaten over and over again? NO. Why did he have to go this far? WHY? I wanted to get right up in his face and scream at him, "WHY are you doing this? WHY can't you just let me go?. JUST LEAVE ME ALONE."

Panic arose within me as the prosecutor walked toward me with a barrage of questions. I was afraid I wouldn't be able to speak in coherent sentences. Eerie laughter floated through the universe in response to my fear. Years of abuse and multiple assault left me wondering if I could keep the details from running together into one great big heap that wouldn't make sense to anyone.

*No one is going to believe you...* the voices taunted.

"Can you please tell the court about what happened on the night of April 18th and next morning of the 19th?"

In a ragged, soft voice, I recounted all of the details I could remember. All I could remember. So many details. Some were vividly clear while others were a blur. I wanted to melt into my seat and just disappear.

When the prosecutor was finished, the defense attorney took a crack at breaking me down with questions about timelines, make-up sex and started calling my integrity into question. Once again, I was portrayed as the bad guy. It didn't seem to matter that I could barely walk after the assault. It didn't make any difference that I had been homeless. The years of bruises and horror stories were irrelevant. Since I had never reported him to the police my story became less plausible somehow.

He asked me to give him precise times that different parts of the attack took place. I couldn't remember. Why couldn't I remember? I felt the panic rising and I feared I would break down on the stand. Over and over he posed the same questions but in different ways. I felt guilty that I didn't know the answers. Finally in my frustration I blurted, "I was being assaulted. I was trying to stay alive. I wasn't watching the clock."

I saw Trooper Ernstes crack a smile and he winked at me, encouraging me that it was going to be okay. I wasn't prepared for this. (Several days later, I remembered that he had taken my glasses early on during the assault. I couldn't have read a clock unless it had been touching the end of my nose.)

The defense attorney went on to badger me about the makeup sex afterwards. The little detail about having to be lifted from the floor prior to having sex was an insignificant fact as he tried to impugn my testimony. I didn't know how to make him understand that I didn't have a choice. Saying 'no' was never an option.

If I had even LOOKED like I was opposed to the idea of sex, the assault would begin anew but ten times worse. It had taken everything I had inside me to keep from passing out from the pain. I was forced to hide the nausea I felt at having sex with the man who had done this to me. How could I say all that to a room full of strangers? Modesty was a form of honor in our religion. My honor was gone. I felt dirty and humiliated. I couldn't force myself to look up and face the blur of faces staring at me. For them, it was someone else's story. For me, it was my life.

When the questions were finally done, I made my way back to my seat in the crowded courtroom. After a few moments to gather his thoughts, the judge made his decision about our case.

"I don't believe Mr. Clemons was trying to kill Mrs. Clemons. I believe he was trying to torment her and scare her with his words and actions. If he had wanted to kill her, he would have done it. Therefore, I am reducing the charge to 'Aggravated Assault with Intent to Commit Great Bodily Harm'."

The charge carried the same prison term, was just one step lower than the original charge, and it was still a felony. One hearing down. I had no idea how many more to go.

I walked out of the courtroom wondering how I was going to ever make it through a trial. The inner turmoil kept me on an emotional rollercoaster. Somehow, I had to control my emotions and keep pressing on in life. Amanda was counting on me. I walked out of the courtroom numb and feeling isolated from the world around me. I doubted I would be able to survive a trial, let alone Amanda. I teetered on what felt like the brink of insanity and feared that any little push would send me over the edge.

## Chapter 7

Manda settled into her new school. We felt so blessed that she had been accepted into a charter school that was part of the public school system. It wasn't well known outside of the local community so I felt she would be protected. I had never heard of it before moving to Holland so I was sure my husband wouldn't know about it or be able to find her there. The school didn't provide any transportation. That was my responsibility and it added to my stress. Not one single day of our new life was easy or without challenges.

The school focused on the arts and was exactly what Amanda needed to thrive. Her art teacher planted seeds of hope that she might actually attend the art school of her choice. Art school was her childhood dream. I had always hoped but was afraid to believe that she would ever have the opportunity to become a designer. She had found her niche and was making friends.

Every day at the insurance agency was a challenge. I felt untrained and very inadequate. My boss had gone through several other office managers who ended up quitting or getting fired. That fact was never absent from my memory. I felt like I was on the verge of getting fired every single day. Finally, she sent me to another agency to learn what I could from an experienced Office Manager. I felt very awkward going to another agency for training. I felt like a naughty child being sent to correctional school. She meant it to be empowering but it wasn't. It was humiliating. I also failed my state exam. Twice. I had one more chance to take the test and pass or I would lose my job.

Trauma, stress, depression, and anxiety played a regular role in my everyday life. I was so afraid I would make a bad decision that I didn't want to make any decisions at all. A notebook became my lifeline of details. I couldn't process everything that was being thrown at me, let alone remember it all. There had not been a single moment of down time, mentally, from the moment we had decided to leave.

Apparently it's true when they say, "the third time's a charm." I finally caught a break and I PASSED the test! I received my license to sell insurance. I was so proud of myself. It was a major accomplishment in my life. One step closer to keeping my job, I knew that even if she did fire me, I would be able to go to another agency and be hired.

I cried myself to sleep almost every night. Nights were the worst. I laid in bed at night and ached to have my soul-mate lying next to me. In the darkness, torment reigned. Thoughts, memories and feelings flooded my heart and soul. Through fourteen years of marriage I had always felt alone. I didn't understand why my body and heart cried out for him. I had begged him to love me. Eventually I realized that he had loved me to the extent that he was capable.

His hurtful words echoed in my spirit, through those long endless nights, "You're fat. No one else will ever want you. No one but a loser will ever want you. You can't make it without me. Whore. Slut." Loneliness filled my heart as my soul cried out to God for mercy.

I struggled every night to fall asleep. I lay in bed every night and watched television until exhaustion would overtake me. I dreaded it. The same nightmare returned night after night. Sometimes a few details would change, but it was always the same dream. We were held captive and unable to escape. Somehow in the dream, he didn't know about our new apartment but we did. We knew what it looked like and what it felt like to live there. It was pure torment to know that feeling of peace and not be able to get to it. Death was more desirable than living in that hell.

It was amazing that we weren't really struggling financially. It was a new feeling. As I paid bills each month and there was money left over it was a stark contrast to our former life. His separate lifestyle consumed quite a bit of our income. Amanda and I were both happy to no longer go to bed hungry or to have to do without things that we needed. It was a whole new lifestyle for us.

Finally, enough time had passed for us to establish residency and our first divorce hearing was scheduled. Once again, I was afraid to go to court. It wasn't going to be pretty. I knew that already. That part was even harder for me as I examined my own beliefs about divorce. My heart was bleeding out as that cord was being cut between us.

Amanda was terrified of seeing her dad again. Just the thought of seeing him sent us both into a panic. Thankfully, the center sent two advocates-- my case manager to stay with me, and a volunteer to stay with Amanda.

My attorney asked the court to grant primary custody to me and his attorney never disputed it. I was stunned. I was expecting a custody battle. He contested everything that had to do with money. He wanted 100% of the house that had first belonged to my family. I was willing to sign the papers to give him the house just so I wouldn't have to deal with him. Thankfully, my attorney kept reminding me about how much proceeds from the house would help us to start over.

The judge ruled that Amanda would be required to complete six counseling sessions with her dad to see if the relationship could be restored. The court would pay for the counseling. We were terrified. Amanda adamantly refused to go, but we both knew she had no choice. My fear was nothing compared to Amanda's. She was a defenseless child without a voice.

My baby, my heartbeat, sunk into a depression like nothing I had ever seen. It scared me to the very core of my being. I couldn't lose her now. We were so close to being free. His family were still contacting her friends at her old school and continued to spew their lies. True love doesn't lash out to destroy a child's spirit and heart.

Shortly after the first hearing, I walked into the living room to find my baby girl curled up into a little ball in the rocking chair, staring off into space, just rocking. I was terrified of what this process was doing to HER. She was the most important piece to this crazy life puzzle, but she was also the most invisible to the courts. It wasn't fair. My first instinct was to run, hard and fast, as far away as we could get from him and his entire family. I called the court appointed counselor and requested an emergency session for Amanda. She needed for SOMEONE to hear what she had to say. I desperately needed someone to be in her corner to fight for her rights and help her get through this ordeal. She agreed.

Amanda and I both knew what the counseling sessions would be like with her dad. I felt horrible that a judge thought it best to subject her to this. He had no idea what he was doing. It wouldn't be a counseling session where Amanda would be able to truly say how she felt. It would be a massive guilt trip about how he was the victim and no one loved him. I felt sick about the whole thing.

We went to several appointments where Amanda was supposed to see her dad and the meetings never happened. After several weeks, I received a call from the counselor telling me that she was removing herself from the case and would be submitting a letter to the court. Someone had called her office claiming to be from a professional office. She demanded Amanda's file and any records pertaining to our case. The conversation didn't go very well. Another occasion my husband showed his true colors to her as well. Her letter to the court stated that she would not be a party to subjecting Amanda to that and she refused to be a part of it. Her recommendation was that Amanda not see her dad until after he had undergone a psychological evaluation. Not a single counseling session ever took place even though we had shown up for every scheduled appointment.

*****

The covering of darkness with abuse is so deceptive that people who live in the light cannot even comprehend the darkness that exists all around them (the lies, the shame and the deception). The evil world of abuse exists parallel with a world of light. When a creature of light exposes the evil of darkness it slithers away to regroup and form a new plan of attack.

*****

At the hearing he was finally ordered to turn over to us all of our belongings including my computer. The computer contained manuscripts I had written and had been in the process of submitting for publication. In frustration, the judge gave them a deadline to deliver the items awarded to me as well as Amanda's furniture and items from her room. A few days prior to the deadline, my attorney called…

"Mary, I'm so sorry. I don't know how I missed this in the paperwork. I thought he was supposed to deliver the items to his attorney's office and you could pick it all up there but that's not what it says."

"What do you mean?"

"His attorney put in the paperwork that you would pick it up at your house." I wanted to throw up.

"How is that possible? I have a protective order. I can't go to the house. I can't go there."

"Do you have someone who can go in your place?"

"I guess I can see if my brothers will go."

"Okay, let me know."

The day of the pickup came quickly. Amanda and I waited at my brother's house while they went to my house to pick up our stuff. We arranged for a civil standby, so that the police would accompany them to the house. They weren't looking forward to the trip any more than I was looking forward to sending them. It seemed like it took forever. Finally, they returned. They were both okay. I was relieved but after I heard their story, I was angry.

Everything we owned had been dumped out in the yard. It had taken so long because only a small portion of our belongings were actually placed in boxes or bags. Porcelain dolls, Barbie's and dresses, art supplies and toys, thrown onto the dirt like trash. Unnamed officers, who weren't supposed to help, picked up baby dolls and coloring books, dusted them off and placed them in the trash bags the boys had taken with them just in case. Our humiliation complete, there on the ground, for anyone to see. The sting of rejection was bitter that day, not in regard to me, but for the little girl who had hopes and dreams of being a princess, his princess.

We received his message loud and clear. Although, technically, he had done as the judge had ordered, he didn't give either of us all of our belongings. I actually received more than I was expecting. I was grateful for that. Amanda however had expected ALL of her stuff. It was fairly obvious someone had gone through everything and picked out what they wanted. I couldn't fix it and I hated it for her. Her hurt ran so deep. I wasn't sure if she would ever recover. Anger simmered just below the surface and it mingled with her hurt. I wanted to just scream at him to wake up and look at what he had done.

Blood and DNA were no match to undo the evil intent of the heart.

*****

Summer turned to fall and time marched on around us. We were slowly adjusting to life without abuse. Our apartment was our sanctuary. We both loved it so much. We were able to decorate it how we wanted. It felt so good to live in freedom. We had freedom to be ourselves, to eat what we wanted, and to dress how we wanted. We were able to choose our own friends. We were also able to determine what church we would attend. I was able to read books again as well. Sometimes we just got in our car and drove just to go exploring. It was amazing. There was nothing that could ever make us go back to the old life. NEVER!

*****

The day of the criminal trial, I dropped Amanda off at school. She was sick with worry. I was, too. My co-workers, her friends from school and their parents were all subpoenaed to testify at the trial. It wasn't going to be pretty. Neither one of us wanted to even go to the courthouse, let alone testify.

I went back to the apartment to get ready. Jan was going to pick me up and drive me to the courthouse. I knew I couldn't do it alone. As I started getting dressed, I couldn't decide what to wear. Tossing outfit after outfit aside, I finally settled on something that seemed appropriate. My nerves were completely shot. I didn't want to do this. I didn't want to go. I didn't want Amanda to go. She was supposed to go to the courthouse the next day for the beginning of the trial. The first step was a hearing for the judge to accept or reject the evidence on both sides before the actual trial started.

My purse slung over my shoulder and keys in hand as I headed for the door, the phone began to ring. I knew I needed to go but something compelled me to answer it.

"Mrs. Clemons?" It was the prosecutor handling my husband's case.

"Yes."

"I have your husband's attorney in my office right now. Your husband wants a plea bargain. What do YOU want me to do? If you want to go to trial, we'll go to trial. If you want me to give him a plea, I'll give him a plea."

There was a God in heaven. I only thought about it a moment. All I could picture was Amanda as I dropped her at school that morning and I knew what I had to do. I had to love my daughter more than I hated him.

"For my daughter's sake, give him a plea."

"Are you sure?"

"Yes. So she doesn't have to testify."

"Okay. I'll keep you posted."

"So, I don't need to come to court today?"

"No, I'll let you know about sentencing."

I couldn't believe it. Relief overwhelmed me and tears flooded my face. I was thankful Amanda was at school and didn't see me. It took a while for me to regain my composure.

I picked her up that afternoon and she had a look of fear on her face when she got into the car.

"It's over." She gave me a blank look. "You don't have to testify. They are giving him a plea bargain."

She burst out in tears, dropping her head down on her knees, she sobbed in relief. I knew, without a doubt, that I had made the right decision. Maybe now we could put it all behind us and begin to heal. We needed to heal. The final divorce hearing was all that was left.

When all was said and done it was never about me. Not for a moment. In my mind and heart, I was disposable. I was not what was of value. She was. She was my heartbeat, the reason I had resisted the pull to end my life on more than one occasion. She was the future. She was the best of both of us. She deserved the very best the world had to offer her.

The future was still foggy. I still had so far to go. We both did. I knew that it wasn't over yet, but one giant hurdle was now behind us. I could actually breathe a little freer.

The day of the sentencing hearing, I was scared and calm at the same time. I had the legal right to choose to address the court if I wanted to, or I could remain silent. I had not prepared a statement and I wasn't sure if I could do it. Jan and I entered the court. I was surprised to see sitting in the courtroom, the sister of a friend of mine, who had also been abused in the past, was there on another matter. A friendly face at least.

No one from the prosecutor's office had warned me of the sentence. I was told what the sentence was going to be as we walked through the hallway to the courtroom. There was no time to process my thoughts, but the sentence made me angry. Fifteen years of assaults, lies, torture, broken promises and betrayal just because he could never believe that I truly loved him? Amanda's wounds ran deep into her soul and I wondered if she would ever heal. We lost everything and he lost the one night that was spent in jail. Charge: misdemeanor aggravated family violence offence. Sentence: one year probation and attendance in a batterer's intervention group.

My anger rose out of the injustice of it all. I blamed myself for all of the years I never called the police. I was angry at all of our neighbors who never called the police. I was angry at all of our family who kept their silence, turned their heads or sided with the one who hurt us.

I wanted to speak to him one last time and tell him what his actions had cost us. I regretted not preparing a statement in advance. I tried to share with the court how fifteen years of abuse had culminated to one misdemeanor conviction and it wasn't fair. It wasn't fair to me or to Amanda. I wanted them to know what it had cost Amanda, but my words came across as trying to impact our divorce case and his custody rights. That was never my intention. I wanted him to know how much he had hurt us. I wanted him to know that I had loved him. Amanda had loved him.

In the eerie hidden stages of life, the puppet master revels in tragedy. With every bond that is broken, between hearts once entwined, society shifts like a riptide under the water, a force unseen and dangerous, changing the core of humanity, one family at a time.

## Chapter 8

Our entire marriage I dreaded every holiday. As the years trudged on, a pattern emerged: Christmas was spent with as little time as possible committed to family gatherings. We would spend time at his family's, sometimes he would give in and go to my family's, but more often than not he would leave and go to his friends. If he wasn't feeling that charitable, we wouldn't be allowed to go see my family without him and so we just didn't get to go at all. What no one else knew was that Amanda and I spent those days at home, alone. Other holidays it just went without saying that he would not be home. Sometimes we would be allowed to go to the store or to rent a movie, but holidays were dreadful, horrible times.

Christmas 2002 was a new experience for us. We were so grateful to have been placed on the shelter's Christmas list. It was a different kind of

Christmas. We got quite an odd assortment of wrapped gifts from the very generous donors. None of the clothes were our style and some not our size. We had a few laughs trying on the clothes to see what would fit. Luckily, there were a few items we were able to exchange at local stores for things that we needed. Without their thoughtfulness we wouldn't have had much of a Christmas. Mom was in Georgia. My brothers had their own families. It felt strange being in a new community all alone. We had Christmas dinner with my brothers' families a few days before Christmas and my aunt and cousin spent Christmas day with us.

It was probably one of the most bittersweet Christmases of my life. We were alone, just as we had been for so many years, but alone was a great place to be. My heart ached for Amanda. She didn't get gifts from all of her paternal aunts and uncles and grandparents like she normally did. I was afraid she would be disappointed but she wasn't. She was as happy as I was to be in our little apartment together.

We found a church we felt comfortable in and attended on Sundays. My aunt and cousin drove to our house on the weekends, and sometimes on Sunday to go to church with us. We didn't feel entirely accepted or at home at this new church, but it was as close as we felt we could get. Those were special times. We got to spend time with family that we hadn't been able to be around much before.

His accusations wore me thin. I waited eagerly for it all to be behind us once and for all. CPS closed their case and the state police closed their file. Trooper Ernstes offered to testify in the divorce trial as well, but it was in a different county and so he couldn't. Having him out of our lives terrified me. He had become our guardian angel. We felt safe with him watching over us.

Finally, the day that we both anticipated and dreaded arrived. D-day. Once again, an advocate was in court with me and another advocate waited with Amanda in a secure waiting room so she didn't have to sit in the courtroom. I was so tired of fighting. I wanted it to be over.

Luckily by this time, I had begun to heal a little and I was not quite as terrified as I was before. I was starting to get angry enough to stand up for myself a little bit. After a year of hearings, I couldn't believe that my attorney had never said a word to the judge about the domestic violence, until now. He had a conviction for domestic violence. That was all that needed to be said. I could see a change in the judge's demeanor, but I didn't know if it would really make a difference.

Finally everything was haggled over sufficiently, the house was ordered to be sold and the judge laughed at my husband for even thinking he was entitled to future royalties for any written work that I sold in the future. He still refused to agree to final terms of the divorce so that it could be settled. There were details in the decree regarding life insurance and something else that would go to Amanda, and he refused to sign the papers with it the way it was worded. The judge granted the divorce in my favor. If my (now ex) husband refused to sign the papers within a specified period of time, the judge would sign it and it would be final. My attorney agreed to draft the final document and submit it to his attorney. Now, I just had to wait those final few days and I would be free.

*****

Tax time rolled around and I was excited. I desperately needed a new car and I was hoping to get enough of a tax refund to put a down payment on a new vehicle.

I sat in the little cubicle at the tax preparer's office and I couldn't believe what she was saying to me.

"I wasn't homeless. I don't understand what you are saying to me. I lived in a shelter for a month but I OWN a house."

"I understand but if you live in a shelter

at all, you are considered homeless. You are exempt from paying any taxes so you get back everything you paid in, in addition to the earned income credit."

It was the most humiliating moment of my life. I had not considered myself to be homeless. I definitely needed the money and I was grateful for it, but I never considered myself to be 'homeless.' However, the tax refund was amazing. It was enough for us to not only purchase a car but also to take a road trip for spring break.

As a teen, my family lived in Texas for a few years. I loved Texas. Moving back to Michigan at seventeen had been a blessing and a curse for me. During the course of the prior year, I had reached out to old friends in Texas and they had supported me emotionally and prayerfully throughout the entire journey. My greatest childhood memories were of our time in Texas and I wanted Amanda to have that Texas experience.

ROAD TRIP.

My life had been so controlled that I had been barely allowed to leave town without an escort. I only went into the bigger towns if I was with one of his family members. The mere thought of a road trip was scary and exciting all at the same time. I even felt some exhilaration feeling as if I was actually breaking the hold he had over me. I felt even a tad rebellious at the thought of driving cross country alone. Negative thoughts whispered in one ear that said I was crazy and at the same time another voice applauded my bravery.

We piled brand new luggage, pillows, snacks and a cooler into our new car and hit the road. "Family Portrait" by Pink blared through the speakers of the stereo, atlas in hand, we headed toward Chicago in the midst of Friday evening traffic. Never in my life had I driven in that much traffic but just as my nerves started to get the better of me, our turn off to go south headed us out of rush hour traffic and toward miles of corn fields in the midst of farm country. We were free. My confidence grew with each passing mile.

We were welcomed in Texas by friends who were really 'family' of my heart. A new beginning brewed in my spirit. Texas wasn't a new place for me, it was however, a safe place. For me: safe was enough.

We had barbeques, toured Dallas, went to Six Flags and Amanda got to make friends with other teens her age. It was healing for both of us. By the end of the vacation, I knew I wanted a fresh start and I wanted to move to back to Texas. Manda was all for it.

The distance between us and him gave us a new sense of liberation. There was no need to watch over our shoulders or peek around every corner. The 911 cell phone lay forgotten in my purse. We could breathe without the shadow of fear lurking behind us. The fresh Texas spring with trees budding new life and excitement for the upcoming summer season was contagious. It spoke of new life to me. HOPE budded fully to life on that week-long excursion to Texas. The time passed way too quickly and before we were ready, it was time to make the return trip home.

The fairy tale neared its end the closer we came to the Lake Michigan shore. By the time we made it back to Michigan, we were both exhausted from the drive and ready for our own beds. However, that old familiar dread began to surface again as I plugged in that silent 911 phone to charge. Insurance, sales, housework and fear resumed their place at the forefront of my mind. Part of me wanted to turn the car around and stay in Texas forever.

Life resumed. Amanda went back to school and I went back to work. The pressures at work increased my desire for a fresh start. I was torn. Amanda had friends at school and her first boyfriend. I wished we could transplant her school and all of her friends with us to Texas. It was the first time in her life she was able to lead a normal life. I didn't want to take that away from her, but I also knew that we would always live in fear if we stayed.

That rekindled romance from my youth also heightened my desire to move. I hated being alone. I had never witnessed a healthy relationship and so my concept of healthy was to settle for whatever attention came my way. Charles seemed safe, albeit there were major issues and challenges we would be forced to overcome. My romantic heart believed that love would conquer all.

I searched the Internet for hours each day looking for every insurance agency I could find within seventy-five miles of Terrell. Each paycheck I mailed a stack of resumes. I searched our company database at work and contacted every one of our offices in my targeted area. Every extra cent I earned was spent on this passionate search for employment. My mind was made up to escape from Michigan and the whole family who had been so intent on destroying us. My goal was to move as soon as school was out so we could settle in over the summer.

The waiting game began. Several weeks passed and the end of the school year loomed before us. Finally, I got not one, but two requests for interviews from two different Nationwide agencies. The problem was, they wanted to interview me in person which meant a flight to

Texas. Around the same time, my friends called from Texas to let me know they had located a duplex for us. The landlord was in the process of remodeling it and it would be ready to move into when we arrived in Texas. He agreed to hold it for us.

"I don't understand why you need to move across the country when you have such a future here." Cindy replied when I requested time off. She wasn't at all excited at the thought of my leaving.

"Cindy, you've done a lot for me and I appreciate it more than you more. I just don't feel like I will ever feel safe here. I'm always looking over my shoulder and I never know when he's going to show up. I really need a fresh start somewhere. I need to fly to Texas for job interviews."

"Well, you can't take off during the week."

"What if I left early on Friday?"

"No. If you're going to do this then you are going to have to do it on your own time. If they are really interested in meeting you, they will meet you on Saturday."

Her lack of support made me angry. I expected her to be relieved that she wouldn't have to fire me. I resented her for making it even harder, but it also made my resolve even stronger. I was going to find a way to make this work. Both agents agreed to give me a Saturday interview.

I left Holland for the Grand Rapids airport about 3:00 in the morning to fly to Dallas. I had never driven that stretch of highway. The airport lights lit up the night sky and beckoned me to make the turn onto the road leading into the airport. Following the signs for parking, I found a space in the long-term parking lot.

Lugging my suitcases behind me I headed for the check in area. I had no idea how to check bags or how to navigate an airport. I was so scared. I had never flown before and I was doing it the first time by myself.

With every step I took part of me wanted to turn around and flee (in terror) back to the safety of my little apartment in Holland. But somewhere from deep within me arose a stubbornness that whispered I would not fail. This new-found quest for freedom spoke louder than the negative forces surrounding me. Every step forward broke another cord that tried to hold me back.

When the call came for boarding I nervously gathered my belongings and headed toward my gate. As I stepped into the plane, I nearly turned around when I saw how small the plane was. I could literally count the seats in about a one minute or less. I was not comforted by the thought of flying on a small commuter plane over Lake Michigan to Midway Airport in Chicago.

When the travel agent booked my flight, I never even thought about what it meant to have a window seat, right over the wing. I watched as the other passengers made their way on board and started putting their items in the overhead compartments and under their seats.

A group of men boarded the plane and several carried guitar cases and it was fairly obvious from their conversation that they were all part of the same band heading to their next "gig." One of the guitar toting men plopped himself down into the seat next to me.

Nervousness must have been tattooed all over my face as he gave me a look of sympathy. He settled back into his seat.

"So where are you headed?" I wasn't sure if he was safe to talk to or not but it was a nice distraction from the sound of the engines starting up.

"Dallas."

"Oh really? What takes you to Dallas?"

I poured out the whole story of domestic violence, shelter, job offers and the hopes of moving for a brand new start. Somewhere in the midst of the avalanche of words, I also shared that it was my first time to fly.

He spent the remainder of the flight sharing

funny band stories and I found that they worked to distract this frazzled blonde from thoughts of a plane crashing into the dark waves of the gigantic lake below.

Charles met me at the airport in Dallas and drove me straight to my first interview. As he navigated Dallas traffic, I worked on smoothing out my rumpled business clothes and smoothed my hair. I was already feeling the effects of little sleep, an early morning flight and a layover in Chicago.

My first interview was scheduled at a Starbucks located a few storefronts down from where the brand new Nationwide Agency was going to be located. It was over an hour from the airport. The agent interviewing me was newly hired by Nationwide himself and hadn't even begun his own training with the company yet. He was hired in the same "new agent" program that Cindy was a part of and so I was familiar with the entire structure of the program, sales and how much work it would be. I knew my experience was a plus because I could already run an agency and he couldn't.

A tall lanky former car salesman, preacher turned insurance agent met me inside of Starbucks. He had a laptop set up. Nervously I took a seat and he began asking random questions about my Nationwide experience and duties. Before I realized what he was doing he whipped the laptop around so I was facing the keyboard and screen.

"Let's see how you can type." He reached down to dig in his computer bag to find something with text on it for me to copy.

The man at the table next to us gave me a look that was half sympathetic to my plight and half in disbelief himself that this man was going to put me through an impromptu typing test in the middle of Starbucks on a Saturday afternoon. We exchanged amused smiles and I started to type. I didn't fly all the way across the country to let a typing test stop me.

I knew before he finished his last question that he was going to offer me a job. If he had his way, I was going to train him how to run an agency. I looked at my watch and realized that we needed to get on the road so I could make my next interview. Together we walked out into the hot Texas sun.

"Mary, I would like to make you a job offer."

"Don, I think you need to know that I have one more interview today with another Nationwide agency."

"What would it take to get you to agree to work for me? I know you need to make a decision pretty quickly so you can relocate."

My heart pounding in my chest, I wasn't sure what I should say to him.

He quoted a salary amount that was several thousand a year more than what I was making in Michigan.

"Can I let you know this weekend before I fly home?" Definitely not expecting a job offer on the spot, I was tempted to say yes right away but I really wanted to see what offer I might get at the next interview.

"I'd really like to settle this right now." Spoken like a true car salesman. I caved. I needed a confirmed job in order to get permission from the court to move.

"Okay, I accept." I decided I could always reconsider if the other agency had a better offer.

Running late for the next interview we headed across Lake Ray Hubbard and into Rockwall for my next meeting. Walking into the building I was impressed. The brick building appeared to be fairly new and was tastefully decorated in Texas style. This wasn't a storefront leased property. This agent had been around a while and was doing well. I was comforted by that fact.

Cindy and Don were both "financed agents" which meant if they didn't meet their sales goals they could lose their agencies and also be unemployed. The sales plan was very rigorous and added to an office manager's stress on a daily basis. A long time existing agency usually had a solid book of clients and the sales came much easier. So did the commissions. The salary, benefits and commission base would definitely be more favorable in an established agency than in a brand new one.

The interview at Stan Lucky's office was much more professional and scripted. I wasn't quite as confident this time. He had the means to hire someone with more experience in the Texas market. I wasn't sure.

As Stan began wrapping up our conversation, "My office manager will be reviewing all of the resumes and I'll have her give you a call next week if she has any more questions for you."

Walking out of the office, I was glad I had accepted the other offer. It wasn't ideal but it was a job offer. Not bad for a single day's work.

Charles turned his truck toward Terrell and we headed down Highway 205 to our final appointment of the day. As exhausted as I was, I really wanted to see the inside of the duplex. I prayed it was in a nice area and suitable to meet all of our needs.

He turned onto a fairly nice residential neighborhood in an older section of town. The other homes on the street were decent and nothing set off any warning signs in my head of danger. The cream colored wood sided duplex was very plain and without much curb appeal but it had a paved driveway, shrubs in the front of the house and it was clean. I was good with it.

The landlord greeted us wearing paint covered jeans. The renovations were still underway.

"Thank you for waiting on us today. I'm sorry we're late. I underestimated how long it would take to travel and make those other appointments."

"No problem. Let me show you around."

I was disappointed at the size of the space. It was definitely smaller than our apartment in Michigan and not nearly as nice but I kept reminding myself that he wasn't through with it yet either.

New tan carpet was laid throughout the duplex. The kitchen and living were combined in one small room. I wasn't at all sure that all of my furniture would fit in the space. The sink, stove, refrigerator and counter space were all in a straight line along one wall. There really wasn't any space for a dining room table anywhere. A decent sized bedroom opened off the living room and faced the road. The only bathroom was in the hallway. The master bedroom was at the back of the duplex and the back door was located inside the master bedroom which opened onto the back porch which was shared with the neighbor.

It wasn't ideal but I knew we could make it

work. It was a start. I knew that once we got settled we could find something else if that place didn't work for us. The rent was also cheaper than what I was currently paying. That was another bonus. I would get a raise and lower rent. I was happy.

"Are you sure you don't mind holding it for us?"

"It's not a problem. It will take us almost that long to finish the remodel."

"Okay. I'll take it."

"Wonderful. I know you said you needed something to take home with you so I brought my standard lease for you to look at." He pointed to paperwork that was laying on the counter.

"The lease needs to be contingent upon approval from the court to move. Do you have any objection to that? I don't want to be stuck with a lease that I can't uphold if the judge says no and I don't want the judge to think I am planning to move no matter what the court says."

"That's fine; we can add that. Not a problem."

I returned to Michigan the next morning with a signed lease and a job offer.

*****

Walking up to the courthouse I dreaded what I was about to face. It wasn't going to be an easy hearing. I knew my ex-husband was going to fight it no matter what. I resented the fact that he even had a say in the matter. I resented the fact that after all I had been through that I had to ask permission of a judge to move my daughter out of state but that was the law.

Once again Jan and a volunteer advocate accompanied us to court. We all anticipated that it would be a long day. I was glad this was my last trip to the witness stand but that knowledge didn't make the task at hand any easier. My attorney had become a friend. I was blessed.

"Does Amanda want to have a relationship with her dad?" asked my attorney.

"No. She's terrified of him."

"Why is she terrified of him? Can you explain to the court?"

"He's mean. He plays too rough and makes her cry and then gets mad at her when she cries."

"What do you mean 'plays too rough'?"

"Well, he puts us both in police holds by twisting our arms behind our backs. He also bites us till he leaves marks. We've both had bruises from the biting. He's twisted her arm behind her back until she's down on the floor crying. He does stuff like that all the time. He says he's just playing. She's scared of him."

"Does your daughter want to move?"

"She does."

"Is there anything else you would like to say about Amanda to the court today?"

"Yes. She is angry."

"Why is she angry?"

"Because she feels like all of these adults have been making decisions about her life but not a single person of authority, throughout this entire process, has talked to her and asked her what she wants. She feels like she doesn't have a voice in her own life."

"That is all, Your Honor." Said my attorney.

"You may be excused."

"I have no further questions, Your Honor."

His attorney called him to the stand.

"Have you ever bitten your daughter?"

"No I haven't. She's a liar. My ex-wife is crazy. She's always trying to make me look bad."

My attorney moved from his seat behind the table and he approached the witness stand to ask his own questions. My ex-husband's agitation was apparent to everyone in the room. I feared that they would believe his story but it didn't take long before his own anger began spewing out for all to see. The judge inserted his own questions and his thoughts regarding my ex's answers was evident in his tone of voice.

"I'm going to call a recess and while we are in recess I want to see Amanda in my chambers."

Amanda was waiting in another room in the

courthouse. I wasn't given an opportunity to talk to her or see her before she was escorted to the judge's chambers. I prayed she would find the strength to actually speak her mind, and I was grateful he didn't make her testify on the stand. The recess seemed to take an eternity. Eventually, he returned and we all took our seats to hear what he had to say about our case. Our future was in his hands.

"I have spoken with Amanda in chambers. I will tell each one of you right now that some of the things we discussed none of you will EVER know. However, Mr. Clemons, I want you to know that I believe you did BITE your daughter. She IS afraid of you. She is also a great negotiator. She and I have worked out a deal as far as her visitation goes with you, Mr. Clemons." The attorney was having a hard time keeping him in his seat.

"She has agreed that you can write her letters. Ms. Clemons, you are required by this court to GIVE her any letters that Mr. Clemons writes to her. Mr. Clemons, you may not call her, you may not show up at their house, you cannot send her an email. You may write her letters and if Amanda wants to, she can write you back. I have also reviewed all of Ms. Clemons's documents, and I am granting her petition to leave the state with the minor child, Amanda Clemons. For whatever reason, she feels like their quality of life will be improved by her accepting this position. Although the increase in pay isn't significant, she has testified that her potential for future earnings is much greater in the Dallas area. Therefore, I am granting her petition to leave the state. Court adjourned."

That was our final hearing. It was over. I didn't have to deal with them anymore. Finally, we could move on. The advocates kept us in the courthouse for a few minutes to give my ex time to leave the area.

As we walked to the van, a car slowed down beside us. Inside was my ex and his sisters. One of his sisters yelled out the window, "Good BYE, A-man-da. I hope you're happy now." The car sped away.

I looked at Amanda. The stricken look on her face pierced my heart. She was their very own flesh and blood, and it was just one more intentional jab to try to hurt us both. She was a child. Once again he was able to dump guilt on our child that wasn't hers to bare. I was resigned to the fact that they all hated me, but I couldn't accept what they were doing to their own flesh and blood. The hardest thing to forgive is an offense against your child. No matter how hard I tried, I just couldn't seem to protect her from being hurt.

Part of the shroud of darkness is those feelings hidden inside that one dares not express for fear of eternal judgment and condemnation. Certain feelings were hidden so far beneath the surface of my conscious that even I did not know they were there, lurking, waiting, and seeing how they could continue to control.

So many choices. All throughout eternity is the infinite struggle of good versus evil... of light obliterating darkness. One decision affects another, and another, until a chain reaction ensues that will either ensnare hearts or set them free. Decisions that have an impact for generations. Human nature urges us to trudge on through life and just "go on" as though nothing ever happened. We pretend by wearing "masks," that we are healthy and whole and that nothing can get us down. We pretend because being real would make us feel vulnerable and exposed. In reality, that ever present puppet master would try to keep us wearing those masks of deception to deceive even ourselves over others. If only we were brave enough to go to those dark places, those places that hurt, and let the light expose the darkness and obliterate it once and for all.

Instead I, like generations who have passed before me, believed that how I was, wounded and broken, was how I was destined to remain. Another deception to keep me bound by my past and emotionally unable to grasp the light in all of its radiant beauty. Although my life was changing course and direction, I still had battles ahead. Some cords were easily broken, but others were silky strands, barely visible in the light. They changed and disappeared at a moment's notice only to reappear in a different form whenever the master demanded....

*Part 2: New Life in Texas*

## Chapter 9

Leaving Michigan proved to be much harder than I expected. We spent nearly every weekend with family doing normal family things. Other family members we were never allowed to spend time with were now included in our everyday lives. We cherished every moment.

Amanda had friends at school and she was falling in love with a boy. She LOVED her school. My heart was torn. It was such a hard decision: to stay or to go. I felt so selfish for wanting to move. She deserved to have stability and all of the opportunities the school provided for her.

Somehow, I just knew that I needed a fresh start. I needed some distance from the memories. I didn't want to live the rest of my life in fear of what was around the next corner. I didn't want to carry a 911 cell phone with me every time I walked out a door. I didn't want to stare out the plate glass windows at the agency, at night in the winter, and wonder what was lurking out in the darkness beyond the glass.

My heart wanted to be away from the snow, the memories, the past, and I knew I needed to make this move.

We both cried as we packed boxes and took the decorations down off the walls. Our apartment was our safe place. It was our home. We both loved it so much. I tried not to let her see me cry but she always heard me through the walls at night. I wanted the chance to see if I could find love for myself, too. I didn't know if that relationship in Texas would work out, but I wanted a chance to try.

*****

I finished my last shift at the office. There was still a lot of packing to finish. My brother Ken and two of his boys were going to make the journey with us. He came the day before to go with me to pick up the U-Haul.

"Do you know how to load the truck onto the car dolly?" The man behind the counter asked.

I had just assumed Ken knew how to do that. It was a "manly" type duty and he was a man. Big mistake.

"I don't know how to do it." I hoped my glare would melt him into a puddle in that moment. How in the world were we supposed to get the truck locked onto that dolly by ourselves? It was closing time and everyone else was getting ready to go home for the day.

"I'm not supposed to do this. It's against company policy but I'll walk out there and show you how to do it." I sighed in relief as we followed him out the door.

After the third time of explaining the entire process to us--to no avail, his exasperation turned to compassion as I stood there nearly in tears.

"I'm not supposed to do this but I'll do it for you." He cautiously looked around to see how many of his co-workers were still on site.

"OH, thank you SO MUCH," I gushed in relief.

"Don't worry about it. Have a safe trip." He shook both of our hands after the truck was secured on the dolly. I breathed a sigh of relief and climbed into the passenger seat.

The next morning was the last day of school. I was supposed to start work in Texas the following Monday. I was scheduled to start Texas training in an agency in Dallas. We had to keep to our schedule or I wouldn't have time to get down there.

Amanda brought her boyfriend and some

friends to the house to say goodbye afterschool. They spent several hours in her room, supposedly helping her finish packing. They weren't getting much packed. I knew her heart was breaking at having to move. I hated it for her. It was one more loss. One more sacrifice on her part, for me. I hated myself for causing this much pain in her life. I wanted so badly for her to have a normal life like other kids.

After a couple of hours, I started getting frustrated because we HAD to get on the road at a decent hour. Opening the door to her bedroom, I stormed into the room.

"Amanda you need to say your goodbyes now! I'm sorry but everyone is going to have to leave now. We HAVE to get this finished. Now!"

"Amanda, I'm not kidding." My last warning. It was overwhelmingly hard to make this final push to load the rest of our belongings into the truck. Our beloved apartment was empty. That part of our journey was over. The safety net of the crisis center was no longer beneath us. It was time to spread our wings and fly. I hoped I would be able to fly because if I wasn't, I didn't know what would become of either one of us.

My two young nephews, Andrew and John, climbed into the U-Haul with their dad and

Amanda and I led the way in the car. We were finally on our way.

The journey to Texas was vastly different this time and not nearly as much fun. We didn't have a cell phone and that made communication between the two vehicles very difficult. Our code was that Ken would flash his lights at me if he needed me to pull over. I was also the only one with an Atlas. Getting separated in Chicago rush hour traffic would not be a good idea.

"Amanda, keep an eye out on them behind us. Help me make sure we don't lose them." As we drove into busier traffic I could feel my blood pressure rising. It never crossed my mind, prior to leaving, that he might need to know where the turn off was that would take us south, especially in multiple lanes of traffic.

Miraculously, we were able to stay together and we continued to drive until I saw the flashing headlights behind me. Ken was falling asleep at the wheel. We needed to find a place to sleep for the night.

I pulled into a truck stop that was well lit and had a lot of car traffic as well as big trucks. Ken pulled into a space next to me. We stretched out in the car the best we could and tried to get some sleep before we started the last leg of our journey.

It was late evening the next day when we finally arrived in Terrell. The sun had already set for the night. I parked my car on the edge of the yard. Charles met us at our new home and helped get the truck off the dolly while I took Amanda in to look at our new home.

She looked around and immediately burst into tears.

I was stunned.

"I can't believe we moved all the way here for THIS!"

I felt sick to my stomach and was devastated. I wanted her to like it. I needed her to like it.

"I think we're all exhausted and need to get some sleep. Hopefully, it will look better to you in the morning." I prayed it would look better to her in the morning because it was all I had to offer her. We didn't have a choice. It was going to be our home.

Charles helped Ken unload our mattresses and the couch so we would all have a place to sleep before he headed home. Amanda and I carried in our luggage and we got ready for bed. It didn't take long before everyone was sound asleep. The long trip had taken its toll on everyone.

In the morning Charles brought some buddies to help unload the U-Haul so we could deliver it to the rental place on time. The next step was to figure out the utilities and all of the logistics of settling in and starting a new job. It ended up being more time-consuming and complicated than I expected due to my out of state driver's license.

Amanda and I both held back tears as Ken and the boys prepared to head home to Michigan. I felt a moment of panic as they were walking out the door. We were going to be truly alone without any family to support us. What in the world had I done?

I was totally unprepared for all of the challenges that would still lie ahead of us. A heart combined with another through a bond of marriage is not an easy thing to overcome. Brokenness was still my constant companion, and although I smiled and worked hard to convince myself that all was well, I still had much to learn about life, relationships and love. Building a new relationship when one hasn't recovered or healed from another can never be a healthy or positive way to live. I had no earthly concept of what that love should actually look like. Boundaries that show respect and care, consideration and trust are precious and should be handled with great care. However, when wounded hearts plunge forward, regardless of the risk, impulsive desires can thwart the greater plan of a master healer who wants to make all things right.

## Chapter 10

Amanda's first day of school was very traumatic and scary. She was harassed the first day by an older boy who was bigger in size and very forward in his manner. She was scared of him and scared of getting raped at school. I was completely floored by this. What had I done? I wanted her to experience the greatness that I remembered. Layers upon layers of guilt continued to pile up in my heart. I blamed myself for every hurt and pain she ever experienced. I couldn't forgive myself for subjecting her to the hell that was our life. I also could not forgive the man who had caused us to flee into this exile from family and friends in order to feel safe.

It was a hard year for Amanda. I had to make her go to school every day, and her grades took a nose dive. My gifted and talented honor roll student gave up. Her hope was quickly fading.

The move was not what I had expected or dreamed of for her.

The loss was too much for her: her entire family, her dad, her friends, a school she loved with a future of college. Emotionally she continued to slip away from me and I didn't know how to bring her back.

Depression sank its dark tentacles into her heart and soul, and threatened to drag her deeper into an abyss of darkness. Those faint glimmers of hope that had sprung to life for her in Michigan began to fade. I was terrified as I watched their embers begin to die one by one. She struggled to make new friends. Her isolated childhood made socializing difficult. The few friends she made also struggled with their own darkness.

I tried to fool myself by reminding myself that we were recovering and moving on from our past. I was functioning, at best, but mostly I was filling my days and nights with as much activity as I could in order to keep the hurt and pain buried as deeply as possible. We started to not spend as much time together and I started leaving her home alone when I went places. I couldn't emotionally deal with the depth of her pain when I couldn't even deal with my own. I didn't know where to turn for help.

My relationship with Charles wasn't turning out to be what I thought it would. Building a life together in reality was much, much different than building it based on long distance dreams. He was devoted to me but he had issues of his own. After just a few months, we began talking about marriage and building a life together. I plunged in head-first, not even considering another option. Dating strangers was terrifying to me. I would never be able to know for sure if any man would be who he claimed to be. Trust did not come easily.

I felt the flutter in my abdomen and knew right away what it was. I had only felt that feeling one time before in my life. I was pregnant.

I stood in the bathroom and held the pregnancy test in my hand. I stared in disbelief at the positive result. Panic rushed over me like a tidal wave. I wasn't prepared to be mom to a brand new baby. I had no idea how I was going to manage all that was already on my plate and a new baby as well.

Later on that day I showed the results to Charles. He was almost giddy with excitement. He didn't have any children. This one would be his first. He wanted to shout the news to the world. I wouldn't let him.

I dreaded telling Amanda. I wasn't sure how she would receive the news. My heart feared she would think I was irresponsible or that a new baby would take her place in my heart. It wasn't an easy conversation to have. The rest of the family also had mixed emotions.

Once the initial shock wore off, an excitement began to take hold in my heart. I had always wanted a son and somehow I just knew that the new life growing inside of me was a boy. Daily life continued on as usual and I soon had to discover ways to make it through the work day with morning sickness and other medical issues from the pregnancy. Nothing in life was ever easy.

Instead of taking time to truly deal with my own pain and issues, I did like millions of others in the world and rushed headlong into this relationship before I really knew what I was getting into. I had been married since I was 19. Charles felt safe. He and his family were familiar and comfortable to me. I had known them since I was twelve. They accepted us like family. I loved them. There were so many issues I needed to work through, but instead of facing my stuff, I kept myself busy from sun up till sun down. It was all pretense, a façade that all was well.

We went to the movies, to the races, or hung out with his family at the lake during the summer. The unrelenting voices whispered in my ear, "Worthless, unlovable, he's going to leave you too, you can't trust any of them...." I tried to let others in but the years of being isolated and alone made it extremely hard to be comfortable in social situations. I failed miserably and hurt people time and time again because I shut them out and separated myself from them. Often accused of being stuck up or thinking I was better than everyone else, it only added to my feelings of worthlessness and that I was too messed up to be a normal person.

Amanda and I continued to struggle with our relationship. She tried to bury all of her past hurts but they still impacted every aspect of her life. We continued to struggle. She needed me to be a mom. And I only wanted to avoid conflict, so I tried my best to be her friend.

We both continued to mask our pain and pretend that everything was okay. Amanda didn't want to hurt me, so she kept things from me. I knew there were secrets that I needed to know, but I allowed her to keep them. It was easier for both of us that way.

She changed a little more each and every day. She stopped wearing pretty, colorful clothes and started shrouding herself in black. She took on a "Goth" lifestyle that I didn't understand. Horrible nightmares plagued her at night. The only way she could get any rest was during daylight hours.

A veil of guilt hung between us that clouded what I could and couldn't see. My love for her constantly battled with my guilt and I completely shut down as her mom. She had very few house rules and little responsibility. I wasn't strong enough emotionally to have any sort of battle of wills with my teen child. I loved her. I wanted to make up for her lost childhood so I tried to do that by buying her material things. She convinced me to allow her to homeschool. I knew in my spirit it wasn't a good idea, but I gave in.

The setting was different and new players had entered the stage of our lives, but minus the physical abuse the choreography remained much the same. Yes, we were safe and yes our bodies were free, but our hearts were still bound in ways we couldn't see. Blindly we went through the motions of life, and life went on grandly around us. However, we were still trapped in the torment of our pasts. We were still controlled by invisible forces and ties that no matter how hard we tried: we could not break free. In sad retrospect, it's almost as if our lives transformed from tragedy to comedy for the evil audience who waited upon the edge of their seats to see how the second act would play out. How the puppet master enjoyed our attempts to break free while we never even realized that he still had us firmly in his grasp.

## Chapter 11

My entire identity was wrapped up in my faith in God and I was plagued with questions. *Was God real? Did He love me? Could I ever be worthy of His love?* I wasn't sure what I believed. My theology was in question and I didn't know any of the answers. Our church had so many rules to achieve heaven's reward, and I struggled with all of it. The biggest issue was in coming to terms with how ugly church people could be to one another. I didn't understand how people could preach from behind a pulpit, teach Sunday school, play an instrument or sing on a church platform and then purposely try to destroy someone's life when they weren't in church. I didn't get it.

The church's code of modesty said that a woman couldn't cut her hair, wear jewelry, makeup or pants. Salvation was dependent upon abstinence from those things. I didn't know who I was as a person or what I believed. I didn't know what kind of clothing I liked or wanted to wear. I had to discover what kind of programs I liked on television and music to listen to. Making my own decisions was a foreign concept. I basically spent fifteen years of my life in isolation imposed by my husband and my church. I struggled to make sense of a belief system that contained facets of stark contradiction.

My long dirty-blonde hair reached the bottom of the salon chair as the stylist prepared to trim it. Sitting in the chair, I struggled to hold back the tears. I wanted to shorten my hair so it was easier to take care of and was more stylish, but part of me was afraid that lightning bolts or something would immediately zap me and send me to straight to hell the moment the scissors touched my hair. Amanda watched from the chair next to me.

"Come on, Mom. Just let her do it." I brushed the tears away quickly, embarrassed by something so silly upsetting me so much.

"Just a few inches. That's all. I don't want it too short." I just couldn't go all the way with it. I couldn't do it. I had to ease into it. "God please forgive me," my heart cried out. I didn't want to go to hell. I didn't want to let him down and I didn't want to cause any angels harm by cutting off my glory. All the scriptures and sermons ran through my head as she cut off the teeny bit I allowed her to. When she was through, I was amazed that I was still alive. I wanted to look like everyone else but the doctrine of our church taught that this very act was one of eternal rebellion that would have greater implications than the simple length of my hair.

My heart was most traumatized by the loss of my relationship with the God I had faithfully served. I ached to know that I was acceptable and loved by Him, but if His people were His hands and feet on this earth, then it was obvious that I was nothing of value or worth to Him. The "church" had not demonstrated His love to us or any love at all. Certainly, we didn't feel mercy or grace. It was not a safe place or a refuge. It was a place of condemnation and hurt piled upon self-righteousness and show. If "Christians" were His representatives, then I no longer wanted to be a part.

Luckily, for me, there is a level of grace that cannot be understood that comes from a place of love so profound that the human mind cannot grasp it. The teaching of my youth had taught me that God was judgmental, and a final reward of damnation and hellfire would be my eternal consequence. However, from somewhere deep within my heart there was a whisper that spoke to those hurt places within, a voice that spoke of life, hope and a greater love. I could not reconcile the things I had learned about God from the church to the things that stirred within my spirit and soul. There surely had to be something more. My heart ached to know real truth and my soul longed for peace and comfort.

Somehow, some way, I had to figure it all out. What did I believe about God and heaven and hell? For some reason, The God of the heavens was silent and not answering my pleas or cries. Trudging on in life, I began to shed the shroud of condemnation and legalism that hung over me.

Somewhere between my head and heart there was a disconnection of the spirit and truth. I couldn't make sense of all of the Biblical doctrine and scripture I had been taught. I couldn't figure out how to apply those beliefs in a world full of injustice, hurt and brutality from one human being to another. Somewhere in the middle there was something that didn't strike a chord of truth. The things I had believed since I was thirteen were securely engrained in my thinking and in every fiber of who I was. It was as if my spirit and body were at odds with each other. A battle was raging around me that I could not see. If somehow the connection of love could be made from my head to my heart, everything would change and I would be free.

I found myself wearing short skirts and low cut tops, just because I could. I lost a lot of weight while we were in the shelter and afterwards. My weight was a constant struggle. I finally felt pretty again, after so many years. My new style of dressing was definitely a far cry from my long skirts and school-marm style clothing from the past. Amanda often shook her head at the clothes I chose to wear and I simply blew her off thinking she was just embarrassed that her mom could pull it off.

It wasn't long before my shape began to change as the new life began to grow inside of me. Amanda was shocked, angry and perhaps a little jealous that I was going to have another baby. She had been an only child for seventeen years. Once I accepted the fact that life was never going to be the same again, I began to get excited about the new baby. I prayed Amanda would eventually come around and accept him too.

Charles and I made plans for our future together. I had doubts about what marriage would be like and many red flags were there, but I felt safe. I ignored the red flags and continued on. He had a "past" and issues that came with it. I thought I could deal with it. I also thought our friendship type love would be able to sustain a long term relationship. We set a date for the wedding and I began to make plans.

One of his bosses invited us to go to church with them. We made excuses for several weeks and then one Sunday we decided to go. It was an experience that would change my life forever. It was a Cowboy Church. I had no idea what that meant.

## Chapter 12

Driving out of our little town on an old country road, it seemed like forever before we pulled up to an old white wooden church building. A cemetery flanked the church on one side, with an old iron fence surrounding it. Cars were parked in the gravel parking lot, on either side of the building, some seeking the shade of trees. I wasn't sure what to expect once we walked inside. We were met with cowboy hats and blue jeans everywhere. It was definitely not what I was expecting. Well, maybe a little.

Our friends greeted us and I was grateful because everyone else just seemed to go on about their business. A few came over and shook our hands. A little while later the service began with country style music and hymns of old. I recognized some of the hymns out of the old Baptist hymnal we were using. They brought me comfort. The memory of twenty years of service in music ministry (on the piano and singing) stung a little bit as I watched the musicians up front. It was hard sitting on a pew instead of being on the stage.

I was somewhat surprised by an old familiar longing to let my fingers travel over that long stretch of ivory. Prior to this day I had spent a year convincing myself that my time of worship was over. God no longer had any use for me or plans for my life. Somehow I had come to believe that the vow I had made, as a young girl, to the God up above no longer mattered—*Lord, if you will just give me the talent to play… I will always play for YOUR glory… and if there ever comes a time that I don't play for your glory, take the talent away from me.*

Through years of isolation at home, my consolation was music. I spent hours and hours practicing the hymns and choruses our congregation loved to hear. Music became my lifeline to sanity and my connection to my Father. My earthly existence consisted of wearing masks concocted to ward off attacks from my husband, or at the very least to protect myself from them. The only time I could ever just truly be Mary was when I was sitting behind the keys of my piano. Worship was my voice. It was the only avenue I had to pour out my heart to the heavens.

As I sat on the pew in that Sunday morning service, with simple country folks, singing along to hymns with guitars and a fiddle, something stirred within me and a longing as old as the ages softly drew me in.

*****

Another week went by and I couldn't get this unique church service off my mind. Everything about that place was raw, basic and simple, from the message to the music to the old-fashioned altar call to accept Jesus into your heart at the end. It was sweet and pure.

I received another invitation and I reluctantly agreed to return. I didn't want to get sucked back into "religion," drama, and the politics of church life. The next time we visited was for the Pastor's ordination service and there was a fellowship dinner afterwards.

Once again, the little band took the stage and I waited to see if someone would take up residence on the bench at the old rickety-looking high backed piano on the stage. It sat there alone and unloved throughout the service. I sat there and envisioned my hands playing along with the other musicians. I constructed chord patterns in my head and hummed a harmony along with them as they sang. I thought about all that I had lost and sacrificed. I still wasn't good enough, or worthy enough, or lovable enough.

When the ordination ceremony concluded, we all departed for the ancient fellowship hall and a typical church pot luck dinner feast. Before too long I started looking for a path of escape from that room full of strangers. Panic and anxiety rose up inside me and I knew I needed a quieter place to hide. I couldn't resist the urge to seek solitude in the sanctuary. The quietness, solitude and familiarity of the altar brought me comfort. It was as if a force more powerful than any other was calling and drawing, in gentle fashion, allowing me the choice of obeying the call or rejecting it. The sweetness of that moment was more than my heart could resist. It was familiar and I recognized its source. I longed for answers and so my heart cried out in the only way I knew how.

Gingerly, I slipped behind the keys of the old rickety piano. Glancing cautiously at the door leading to the fellowship hall, I prayed that the sound would not travel through hundred year old walls and the moment would be mine alone.

I had not played in such a long time that the sound was rusty and full of mistakes but it brought more than just a little joy to my heart. Several stanzas and choruses later and I suddenly noticed a tall, lanky man leaning across the top of the piano. Embarrassed, I resisted the urge to flee.

"We have band practice on Monday nights." His gentle eyes and calm demeanor helped me get past my embarrassment at being caught on the stage without permission.

I stared at him blankly, not quite sure what he was saying.

"You should come practice with us. We don't have a piano player."

I didn't want to be rude and just say no. Part of me was screaming, "YES." Churches don't just ask total strangers to join their worship team. Especially strangers who aren't even members of the church. He didn't know who I was or what my past was or that I was carrying a baby inside me and I wasn't married. He didn't know that I knew better. If he knew all those things, he wouldn't have extended the invitation, because that isn't what church people do. I wasn't good enough to play that old piano. Especially not now.

I made up excuses.

"Well, just think about it and if you change your mind, the invitation is open."

That Monday night, I was at band practice. As I drove to the church, I nearly turned around at least three times. I sat outside in my car for a while, afraid to go in. What if he had changed his mind? I was going to look stupid walking in like I belonged there. Who did I think I was anyway?

It took a force greater than myself to make me walk through those doors and into the building that night.

"Hey... Come on up here." I was greeted with smiles and a few odd looks, but everyone was happy to have a piano player on board. My skills were not the best and the old piano was slightly out of tune, but sitting on that old bench felt like I had come home.

*****

Cowboy Church life was different than anything I had ever known. The church environment for sure was different. The music was not the Pentecostal style I was used to. However, I loved the sense of community and family I felt in this group. Some were friendlier than others, I must admit. However, the thing I loved the most was that among the band members, I was accepted.

As the church continued to grow and plans were made to purchase a local arena, the band also continued to grow. We added a new worship leader and several other musicians. Still very shy and insecure, I continued to lay back and let others take the lead. I was perfectly fine with that. It was what I was used to in church anyway. I loved singing harmony parts and filling in the musical gaps. However, there came a Sunday when I really wanted to share a song that I had written and I sang it as a special. Somehow, the emotion of what the song meant to me rang through to the ears of other band members and a new era in my life was born.

A couple of the band members teased me afterward. "I think we've been missing something here. A diamond in the rough." They laughed and teased. Totally embarrassed, I tried to blow them off.

"Y'all are crazy."

"Nope. I think we are going to be hearing a lot more from you."

I shook my head and walked away. There was no possible way I was singing any more leads at church. NOPE. Not a chance.

As we added new music to our repertoire, lead parts seemed to come my way. I was so nervous, I couldn't sing with all my heart. Our worship leader, Brian, stopped us all from playing, as he calmly looked at me to say, "That was good but I want you to sing it again and this time, I want you to sing it without fear."

Groaning in frustration, I tried the song again, convinced that I would fail. I was not a singer. I was just a "hack" on the piano. No great talent here… please, keep the train a movin'. But, that was not to be. Over and over, he would make me re-sing my parts until I was sure the rest of the band was ready to string me up or cast me out. Every time, he spoke the same words into my spirit, "…sing it again and this time, sing it without fear."

Ever the wallflower, full of shyness, I became nearly ill every Sunday as the task of reading church announcements had somehow become my responsibility. I was not used to such attention, playing lead on piano or especially in singing. These tasks were quite traumatic at first. Soon, however, as my voice grew in strength so did the voice of my heart.

As the evil puppet master began to lose his power in his great quest to vanquish my soul, forces of light began to overtake the darkness. Who would have thought that a road-weary musician, tired from life's battle himself, would surrender himself to lead a raggedy bunch of wannabe musicians in worship and that his simple message would speak to my little girl heart who had never lived a day of her life without fear. "Sing without fear," was spoken as encouragement, but gave voice to the voiceless and helped to set this captive free.

## *Chapter 13*

Work, band practice and preparing for the delivery of my son became all-consuming endeavors. Church once again took center stage in my life and I accepted a team leader role as well. I hid myself in busyness.

Even as I found ways to break free from the ties to our past, Amanda was held even more firmly and painfully in its grasp. Her father's DNA ran darkly through her veins and those ties were stronger than life or death. Every day, I checked on her as often as possible from my desk at work which was almost forty-five minutes away. I was terrified of losing her, forever. My baby girl was defenseless to fight back and the darkness of her world was a place I could not reach. She wouldn't let me into the true depths. I stood on the outside, searching for solutions, but in my still-broken mindset I had no help to offer.

I wanted to give her another chance at childhood with sleepovers, friends, and girly days out, but I couldn't. The chance for all of that was gone. She was in the precarious stage between leaving her childhood and becoming a woman. The father of lies had convinced her that her life had no value or meaning. I never knew until years later that all throughout her childhood, her father had whispered those words into her ear in the shadows of darkness. He blamed HER for the atrocity that was our family, which caused a great abyss of loneliness and self-condemnation to grow within her heart.

The last few weeks of my pregnancy my feet and legs began to swell. I didn't feel well at all. Even simple tasks became a struggle. Don was not very happy about the situation and didn't hold back with his comments. I was stressed over the amount of work I had at the office. My short-term disability coverage at work helped but it wouldn't cover all of our expenses during my leave.

"Well, my dear, it looks like I am going to be forced to help you out." my doctor said as she reviewed my stroke-level blood pressure results. She scribbled out a doctor's slip requiring strict bedrest for the remainder of my pregnancy. I was relieved and scared.

Mom made the trip from Georgia to be there

for his birth. Her timing was perfect as she was there to help me those last few horrible days of pregnancy. Most of my time was spent between the bed, a recliner and the bathroom. She helped me navigate from one location to the other.

A week after my due date, we spent a Sunday morning in the Emergency Room. The doctor determined it was a false alarm and sent me home. Monday morning came bright and early. I was still uncomfortable and felt like the hospital should have admitted me but I had a doctor visit already scheduled that Monday. After a quick exam my doctor sent me straight to the hospital so they could induce my labor. Her conclusion was that my water had been leaking all weekend and she was concerned about infection setting in. It was a dangerous situation for the baby.

Induced labor is probably the most agonizing kind of pain that no words can describe. Mom drove me to the doctor's office and then on to the hospital. She sat with me through twelve agonizing hours of hard labor. Her presence brought back a sense of family that we had lost and gave us a sense of security.

I called Charles at work on my way to the hospital. He checked on me once after he got off work. Then he went home claiming that "it was still going to be a while." For the next several hours, I continued trying to call him to see where he was but he never answered his phone. I felt very abandoned and let down that he wasn't there with me. I understood his circumstances and reasoning, but it didn't change the fact that he was not there. Another disappointment from a man. Finally, as final preparations were under way for delivery, only five minutes before my son was born, Charles strolled into the room with take-out food in hand. I wanted to choke him. Literally.

The nurse handed him first to Amanda. I wiped away my own tears as I saw her tears. She stared at the squirming bundle in her arms. My heart swelled as I watched her hold him. There was healing in that moment. I knew everything was going to be okay. Although his conception and birth would be considered "a sin" or "mistake" by some, to me he was proof that somewhere in the universe, the creator of life had heard that still, small cry of my heart and granted me the desire of my heart: a son.

Mikyle James changed our lives forever. Charles was ecstatic to have a son. Mikyle became "Bubba," (as is only fitting for any Texas-born male child) within the first minute of his life. Life as we knew it would never be the same. It had been a long time since I had taken care of a baby, and now I was a single mother taking care of this one.

The first week at home was rough. I was truly thankful to have my mom's help as I recovered. My blood pressure and health were still a slight issue and help was definitely needed. I spent hours holding him, even while he slept. He owned my heart.

The following Sunday the church broke out into a chorus of "oohs" and "aahs" as I carried him down the center aisle to our seat. I thought my heart would burst. Amanda was the only thing missing that Sunday morning.

Some at church felt I shouldn't be allowed to be on the platform since I had a baby out of wedlock. I felt the sting of their hateful barbs. My decisions were not always wise or informed or right. I wasn't a perfect spotless "Christian" who could live up to the scrutiny of many. I was a wounded, broken soul seeking refuge from a world that had battered my spirit and soul to the point where hope was lost. However, it was in that little country cowboy church, full of simple country folks who were flawed and scarred themselves, where a healing balm began to flow.

Somehow mercy found a home in that little cowboy bunch. They presented to me a way of life that was simple, without fuss or frazzle. No one there was spotless or worthy. Everyone had their own story to tell. Misfits gathered from all around to worship with our raggedy crew. The altars were full and the baptism line would baffle the mind. It was a different way of life.

Through a friend at Cowboy Church, Amanda began to find her own healing. The depression began to lift and color began to fill her life again. It brought me to tears to watch her overcome her fear of horses and participate in a horsemanship program at the church. Everyone kept telling me there was healing in loving a horse. I wouldn't have believed it, if I hadn't seen it with my own eyes. She learned to groom, saddle and ride a horse and of course she picked the oldest, most wounded horse in the arena to love. His name was Old Man and he had only one eye. A bond was formed between them and she made my heart proud.

New life was all around us. Texas was proving to be a good move after all. I knew we weren't completely past the tough times but I knew we were definitely on our way.

From the time Amanda could use crayons or pencils she spent hours drawing in the margins and covers of coloring books. We bought her pack after pack of paper instead and an artist was born. From the time she was little, I told her she could be anything in this world she desired to be as long as she was willing to work hard. Throughout all of our years of abuse, I spoke those words into her life, but in my heart I wondered how it could ever be, considering the fact that her dad would never support her dreams.

*****

At seventeen, Amanda took her GED and passed. Then she started her first year of college. Art school was *extremely* expensive, but a conventional school was out of the question. It was time for me to step up and put my money where my mouth was. I wanted her to know how much I believed in her dreams so I signed the papers for my first parent-student loan to fund her college education. The investment in her was my heart's way of trying to show her she had value and worth, that I believed in her and I believed in her dream.

I drove her to school in Dallas for an entire year before I went to work. Then I would drive back to the school on my lunch or after work to pick her up depending on her schedule. I would pick her up and take her back to my office and her boyfriend would take his lunch break and come to my office to take her home. We did this until I couldn't keep up the pace of it anymore. It began to be too much with a baby at home. It was a hard time on all of us.

*****

After Mikyle was born Mom went back to Georgia, packed up her stuff and moved to Texas. She moved in with us and helped me immensely. It was an adjustment for all of us, but life started to feel a little more normal having my mom around.

Amanda moved into an apartment in Dallas with friends so she was closer to school and rode to school with other nearby students. The adjustment was tough for me. I couldn't wrap my mind around the fact that she was growing up. Letting go was hard. I still wanted to protect her from the world.

My relationship with Charles continued to decline, and I knew that I could not marry him. Earning the nick name "runaway bride," I broke off our engagement twice... both times, just days before the wedding. They were not my proudest moments.

Making the decision to be a full time, permanent, single mom was not easy. Words from my past echoed in my head as I struggled through the decision making process. Old religious teaching said that if you got pregnant, you married him and made it right. End of story. I just couldn't bring myself to do that. Although I felt great love for him, it had turned more into a friendship kind of love. Our families would be forever entwined and that cord would never be broken, but my heart did not love him in the same manner as lovers. My rash decision to rush head long into love would forever impact my beautiful young son. I could not change my past mistakes or decisions, but I could move forward: wiser, better, and a little more whole than I was before through this hard, but necessary decision to move on in life alone.

## Chapter 14

No matter the chaos of life, time marches on. Amanda pursued her future. Mikyle continued to melt my heart and challenge me with his busyness. My determination to be successful in life and business continued to drive me forward. I thrived on the challenge of selling insurance and watching our agency grow.

I appeared to have it all together. I had overcome. I survived, but secretly behind the walls of my heart, the banner still waved: "DAMAGED GOODS." I wanted to let people behind the wall but I didn't know how to let them in.

I put on a grand show of normalcy and calm, but on the inside a war of emotions and battling thoughts raged. The devastation of life would nearly break me on a near-daily basis. My stubbornness and tenacity to prove to my ex that

I COULD be successful was the driving force that kept me going from day to day.

Amidst the darkness in my private thoughts, a gentle breeze began to blow into my spirit. The yearning for the God of my childhood beckoned for me to find that secret place, a hiding place, where my soul could cry out in honesty and grief.

Friends invited me to events, barbeques, and holiday gatherings, but try as I might to fit in, I always felt an outcast. Unwanted. A bother. I attended the events that were obligatory and made excuses for others, grieving silently at home that I still couldn't break through the wall. It was as if the wall was made of clear glass, miles thick. I was on the inside looking out at the world going on around me in every direction. There were places in the glass where I could venture further and participate, to an extent, with the world but still never entirely free to be me. The wall kept me separate.

I was on a continual quest to prove to everyone, but mostly myself, that I was lovable, acceptable and worthy. I thought I could do that through "works." I was part of the core group and my hand played a role in every activity at the church. I desperately wanted to have friends. I thought their acceptance of me showed love until I reached a breaking point. I had extended myself beyond the scope of my ability to manage and was forced to start saying no.

Guilt plagued me once again as I was forced to step back from being as active in church. I stopped being the go-to person. My phone stopped ringing off the hook. A new kind of hurt began to build and I built another layer around my heart. It seemed that for every step forward, I took ten steps back.

Still the gentle breeze continued to blow in my heart. With every set-back came an epiphany moment of healing and change. The one thing I did not doubt was my great love for my Heavenly Father. My heart longed for the days of my youth when I could pray for hours and stay lost in His presence.

A gentle nudging in my spirit kept calling me to go back to those times of prayer and seek the face of my Father in that secret place. I could not resist that call and so for the next year I devoted my evenings and weekends to Bible study and prayer as I fought through the raging storm in my heart to find my purpose and calling.

As I prayed, through His gentle grace and mercy, He reminded me of a time one year before my escape of the moment when my purpose was revealed to me through a series of dreams. At the time I had no revelation of the true extent of His revelation. In my humanness,

I could not see the greatness, or the majesty, or the mercy. I could only see that I was not worthy of what He was showing.

God, in his great wisdom, speaks to each of us in the way we need to hear. For me it was a series of dreams. He knew that my subconscious mind could and would not be able to grasp the greatness of this call but my spirit self would embrace the sweetness of His presence.

*The first dream led me into a massive congregation in the midst of a great revival. The crowd could fill several stadiums or convention centers. The blend of beautiful voices, both angelic and human, beckoned the very presence of the Almighty to hover over us in His great majesty. His presence was overwhelming, powerful, and sweet. Words cannot really express how great my desire was to remain in that place of holy worship. Then I was totally amazed to find myself standing behind the podium and delivering words of great wisdom and revelation to the massive crowd. My own soul was amazed at the anointing and revelation that was flowing from my mouth like a smooth flowing river of life. There came a moment in time when I was then separate from myself and watching the scene before me. I could see myself preaching the Word and speaking life into those lives before me. Most of all, I felt such an overwhelming sense of peace and love that I knew I never wanted to leave. In another moment, my subconscious mind recognized that I was dreaming and about to wake up. A sadness filled my entire being because I knew that I was where I wanted and needed to be, in the very presence of my Holy God.*

The second dream was much the same as the first.

*The third time I had this dream, I was standing behind the pulpit and I was sharing my experiences with domestic violence. I couldn't hear the words that I was saying but I knew that I was supposed to use my story to help other women who were being abused. I could not see the back of the great room we were in. It was as if the faces became a sea and they extended back beyond the scope of my vision. It was too great a possibility for my conscious mind to receive and even in my dream I became agitated and alert.*

*I awoke to find myself lying in my bed, alone. I looked around my bedroom and evidence of my husband was everywhere in the room: clothes, guns, gun cabinet, knives.... A sinking feeling settled over my spirit.*

*"WHY WOULD YOU DO THAT TO ME?" I cried out to the Creator. "TAKE THAT DREAM OUT OF MY HEART. IT'S NOT FAIR. THE ONLY WAY I'M LEAVING THIS HOUSE IS IN A BODY BAG."*

*Anger began to rise in my spirit because it wasn't fair. I had given up my dreams for a hope and a future and the God that I adored was tormenting me with a hope that could never be mine....*

The stirring in my spirit kept whispering words of hope into my heart: "loveable, worthy, accepted. Mine." I continued to study the Word and to allow His truths to wash over my soul. For an entire year, I sought to stay in this place of growth, of healing.

As I began to reach out into the community, I felt my calling was to volunteer at a shelter and give what I could to help others. I was deeply saddened to find there wasn't a crisis center anywhere in our county and I was forced to extend my search beyond our local community.

The New Beginning Center in Garland, Texas became my place to volunteer. I attended their volunteer training and began to help solicit donations for their annual fundraiser. Even though I knew that it was a worthy help to the cause, it wasn't fulfilling the nagging urge in my spirit to do more.

My evening study time started to take a turn and became long nights of research and dreaming. What if... I started my own program? What if... I started my own non-profit? Pages of a notebook began to fill as I researched how to start a non-profit. I looked for curriculum to use to teach women how to live independently after leaving an abusive partner. It was certainly a book of dreams, for my head kept telling me it was never to be.

Oh, but the Creator of the universe knew more than I and I'm sure He sat back upon His throne and chuckled as He watched me study. I still had no reason to think that it would ever be anything but a dream, but certainly angels were dispatched by the Father to do His bidding and aid me in my cause.

My purpose and calling were ordained in Heaven long before I was ever born. He knew me by name, from my mother's womb. Why would I ever doubt that His plan for my life was greater than the plan my human eye perceived?

There is a secret battle that continuously rages on, behind the scenes, seeking to destroy all that is good, holy and just in this world as well as those who dwell in it. The puppet master continues his scheme to destroy families, lives, hearts and spirits just to feed the ego of one who had already lost the war. Even as hope overshadowed darkness in my life, at times doubt flooded my spirit in vicious waves trying to convince me that hope was just a lie.

## Chapter 15

Even in the midst of my journey, God blessed me with opportunity to share my journey with others. Ladies' ministry was a great source of blessing to me. I loved the ladies of our church. They were precious.

I was invited to share my story at a ladies' night at church, and afterward I met a fellow survivor. The soul connection was instant and we felt as if we had known each other our whole lives. We spent many hours on the phone after that night and a bond was formed between us.

Our friendship led us to start a support group for victims and it quickly snowballed into the development of a brand new non-profit organization: Healing Hearts Ministry. The blessings began to flow so quickly, we could not keep up with it all. We opened an office and began developing crisis intervention services for victims of domestic violence and sexual assault.

Within the first year of operation, we received a miraculous grant that allowed me to quit my job at Nationwide and both of us went full time in ministry with a salary. God moved heaven and earth on our behalf. Volunteers flocked to support us and our community embraced our efforts. We were humbled and amazed at how quickly it all exploded.

We worked tirelessly. The sacrifices we made were great. We called on every business and agency from one end of the county to the other trying to garner awareness for our cause. Year two and three were equally as difficult as we developed programs, forms, grant applications, sought speaking engagements to spread the word. Victims came to us for assistance.

We were known as the domestic violence ladies. The local paper frequently ran stories about the work we were doing. Everyone knew who we were. God was merciful to us. Hundreds of victims passed through our doors for help.

I struggled every day to recognize my value and worth to my heavenly Father. I continued to 'settle' in relationships and accepted emotional abuse from others. The knowledge was in my head but the struggle was receiving it into my heart.

"Mary, you should make a CD," a friend declared to me one day.

I looked at her incredulously. "You have got to be kidding," I replied in disdain. There was NO WAY anyone would want to buy my music. I was barely comfortable singing a solo in church.

I laughed it off and didn't think anything else about it, but the encouragement didn't end there. It quickly became more than a casual conversation, as thoughts of a CD as a fundraiser for the ministry began to take shape. It looked like I wasn't going to have a choice.

Once again the supreme master, Father God, showed His power and authority and the CD project was fully, 100% funded through donations in our community. I was humbled and in awe of the opportunity to go into a studio and actually record.

Music is not just singing for me. It's a deep, heartfelt expression of my great, unending love for my Father. With each note that I sing, I pray God hears the intent of my heart and that others would draw closer to the Almighty and feel HIM in a way like never before. It was almost surreal to think that I was going to be able to make a CD.

I prayed over each song and practiced at home, without a microphone, and sang along to the tracks played through a cheap CD player in my bedroom at night.

Nerves nearly got the best of me as I walked toward the studio door. Royel, the studio engineer, greeted me and ushered me into the sound booth. After a quick prayer, he showed me the process to record music and we went to work.

After the first song, "Word of God Speak," Royel played it back through the speaker for my critique. As I heard my voice, I couldn't believe the voice I heard was my own. I couldn't believe it was really happening.

The sweet presence of the Lord filled the room and my heart as tears began to stream down my face. He wrapped me in his love. Time stopped in that moment as His loving words coursed through my soul.

*"I am a rewarder of those who diligently seek me and for all the years that you were faithful, I am giving you a voice. You will be a voice for those who do not have a voice."*

The tears flowed stronger, and my spirit replied, "Father God, I'm so unworthy. I'm so grateful that You gave me a voice and I am grateful that I am able to turn around and give it back to You in worship."

In that very moment a crack formed in the glass wall that surrounded my heart and soul. In all of my efforts to keep out the world that could hurt me, I had also successfully kept out the Father who created me. This crack did not penetrate the entirety of the wall but for that day, it was enough.

## Chapter 16

The ministry continued to grow at a rapid pace. We struggled to develop the foundation to support the growth and weight. It impacted the work we were trying to do and caused us to falter in our path.

I struggled with being alone and not in a relationship. I still did not know what normal was supposed to look like in a relationship. My head knew that a physical relationship between a man and woman was only meant for marriage, but as much as my heart wanted to do what was right there was an almost physical drive that convinced me that sex equated affection. I didn't know how to receive one without the other.

Oh, how the lies from that unseen deceiver continued to wreak havoc in my life. As I continued to search for real love, I also continued to form those unseen bonds by giving men rights and access to my heart and soul that they did not have a spiritual right to. I could count on one hand all the men I had dated in a period of nine years. Each relationship continued to steal from the true love relationship God intended for my life. I made another serious, tragic relationship mistake that hurt, not only myself, but everyone else around me and impacted our ministry as well. It was almost as if during the entire relationship I moved through life in a trance. Then one day I woke up, the blinders fell off, I saw the relationship for it really was, and I ended it.

Guilt and shame plagued me again as I was now a ministry leader and very well known in our community. My heart and intentions were right. My desire to be pleasing to my Father drove me to continue trying to be righteous, to be good enough. Continuously, I failed. On my own, I could do nothing.

Several years into the ministry, after the addition of employees, one alarming day brought with it the loss of a grant that affected salaries. We, as the leaders, chose in that moment to surrender fifty percent of our salaries in order to keep all of our employees. I determined that I would trust God and continue on. The weight of that decision was hard to bear, considering I wasn't sure how we would make it through.

It was a scary time in my life as I always struggled in trusting God in my finances. The panic would often overtake me whenever something would go wrong; a flat tire, a medical issue or anything else could deplete my funds and would cause me to melt down inside.

God was slowly revealing Himself to me and also healing my heart. I determined that I was going to stay positive, consistently pay my ten percent tithe to my church and trust that God would make a way. The very first month, I lost the child support for Mikyle because his dad went to prison, but I also paid the last payment on my van which balanced out that loss.

I learned so much about faith and trust during that six-month period of time. Every time a bill came due that I didn't have funds to pay, someone at church would come up to me and say, "God told me to give this to you." and it would be the exact amount of the bill, or someone would bring me an item that I needed and give it to me. Our way of living never changed during the entire time. We never went without. I was still able to go out to lunch with the girls in the office and nothing much really changed.

Christmas was drawing near and we still hadn't secured new funding. I didn't know if I would be able to provide a Christmas for the kids. However, just in the nick of time, a new grant came through which covered our lost expenses from the old grant and reimbursed us each for three months of our lost salary, just in time for Christmas.

Much later, God used this experience to heal me from my panic attacks in daily life. There came another time when I grew weary of the constant upheaval of spirit every time something went wrong in my life. My car had broken down and I didn't have the funds to have it repaired. I completely melted down. Again. I prayed for God to reveal to me the source of my panic so I could, once and for all, deal with it. God is faithful. He revealed to me why I melted down over every day occurrences in life. I was broken and made whole in one simple revelation.

I learned a valuable lesson about myself. I mixed faith and trust together. I assumed that I trusted God because I had faith, but what He revealed to me was something entirely different. I had faith that God could move mighty mountains and do anything... but I had faith that He would do that for anyone else in the world... but me. Somewhere along the way, through the years of abuse, it became engrained in the fabric of my being that God didn't love me as much as He loved everyone else. I cried out to Him to rescue me in those darkest of nights, and no matter how loudly I cried for Him to send me help, to deliver me, help never came. How could I trust a trust a God who would allow all of those horrible, unspeakable things be done to me?

The Word told me to trust Him, but the abuse taught me to trust no one... not even the One who created the very DNA of my existence. I realized that He wasn't an "absent God." He was ever present. I could have left at any time and He would have made a way. I chose to stay. I realized that every time I cried, He gathered my tears in His hands. When I was broken, He lifted me up. When I couldn't find strength for another day, He carried me. All of those things: YES. Abandoned me? No.

As lies are exposed and obliterated the cords of the past become broken. The wall around my heart shattered into a million pieces, and I knelt in the midst of the shards of my hurt and let the healing waters reach the deep places that had been hidden for too long.

It was that moment, in my brokenness, that my spirit man also became whole. The cords that held me in bondage no longer had any hold on my life. I was a slave to the lies and abuse of my past, and that day I rose up from the midst of the past, a new creation, no longer a slave to those old hurts but a daughter of the Most High God.

## Chapter 17

### 2010

The mind is a funny thing. Healing is never absolute. Every moment of reflection and growth brings a new level of spiritual responsibility. My heart continued to revel in my new-found relationship with the Father, but my relationships with others still faltered and failed.

No matter how much I wanted to have close friendships and a true love of my own, it just didn't seem to be in the Grander Scheme for my life. I had come so far and overcome so many hurts and obstacles, but still the negative thoughts swirled in my heart and mind, "Too damaged for anyone to ever love you."

I had a full life. Speaking and singing engagements filled my free time, the ministry continued to grow. We were helping people although we also had some internal struggles that played a huge role in where I was emotionally.

I spent my evening hours curled up on the couch with the remote control to the television, my laptop and a blanket. Facebook opened up a social world that I didn't possess in real life. I watched other people share their relationships and explorations of life while I stayed, safe and secluded, on my couch at night. A friend tried to convince me that once I became totally comfortable living on my own and being by myself that God would send my future husband into my life. I didn't believe her. I was convinced that perhaps it would be better if I just never remarried. I didn't believe I had anything to offer as a wife. I was still too broken.

I started searching Facebook for old friends from high school to reconnect with. I had two friends in particular that I really hoped to find: Barbara and Susie. We had been best friends until I moved away after our sophomore year. I thought of them often throughout the years. I found Barbara within the first couple of days searching and she helped me contact Susie. Within a few weeks I was Facebook friends with a good portion of the Terrell High School Class of 1986. I had never been a part of a community before, and the way Terrell and its citizens embraced me added to my healing journey.

As I scrolled through my newsfeed, I noticed one school mate kept posting about his obvious divorce. I could literally feel his pain. Some of his posts were difficult to follow because I didn't know his story.

It was crazy, I knew, but I just couldn't resist the magnetic draw I felt to go and look at his page and picture. The butterflies, the melting in my heart, I knew it was silly to have a schoolgirl crush at my age but I couldn't help it. Kevin Farmer melted my heart with his hazel eyes.

My daydreams told me there was hope, but my heart cried out that he would never have anything to do with someone like me. Emotionally, I was still that high school wallflower that was constantly passed by, unnoticed, by the popular boys.

His dry, cynical humor was hard to decipher from time to time. I was never sure if his posts were serious or his painful attempts at humor. I, sometimes, would join the ranks of former classmates and comment on his posts, but mostly I sat back and watched, without any expectations until the week before the Daytona 500....

*Getting divorced has dramatically changed my life. I spent last Sunday, my 20th anniversary, by myself.*

*Now, here comes Valentine's Day, and I'm reminded again of my divorce. So, think about poor Kevin, alone on Valentine's Day, without a sweetheart. It's going to be so lonely. Just me ...*

And the post stops with the all familiar blue type that says: (See more). I and all of our classmates were forced to click the button to see more to finish reading his post…

*And 250,000 OTHER REDNECKS AT THE DAYTONA 500! WOOOO-HOOOOOOOOO! GO JUNIOR!!!*

I laughed until tears streamed down my face.

I went back to that post and re-read it every day for several days and laughed every single time. Laughter is a healing balm. It's good for the soul. It's good for relationships. It's good for marriages.

"Once again I'll be performing on stage at the Terrell Heritage Jubilee… Stop by and see me." I hit the "post" button and continued on with my online marketing. Managing the entertainment stage was something I did as a chamber volunteer and I loved it. I also enjoyed getting the opportunity to sing for the hometown crowd as well. I love our community.

Suddenly a chat message popped up on my screen from Kevin Farmer. I stared at it in disbelief. "We are going to come, stop by to meet you and hear you sing at Jubilee…."

Heart pounding in my chest, I knew this message must be a mistake... but how could it be a mistake? How many other people from our friends list were singing on the stage? Well, that answer was easy... DUH! NONE! I knew because I booked the talent.

"Awesome. I'd love to meet you."

Such a simple exchange of words, but I couldn't slow down the beat of my heart. This simple exchange of private messages led to more in-depth conversations that kept me hovering near my computer.

I assumed the "we" was his little girl that he posted pictures of constantly. It was obvious she was the light of his life, and that made him even more attractive in my book. He constantly posted pictures of the two of them making silly faces at the camera, and making great memories together. I was mush.

He posted pictures of them at our local ice cream shop, and he was literally only two blocks away from my house. I couldn't resist from sharing that fact with him online.

"Well, come on ...," he replied.

I toyed with the idea of jumping in the car, racing to Braum's and stalking him but I didn't quite have the courage.

After a while, he posted, "I waited in the foyer for an hour like a Walmart Greeter, nodding and saying, Hi, welcome to Braum's." I never was quite sure if he was joking or not.

Amanda started experiencing some health issues and wound up in the hospital for an unexpected surgery. Since her fiancée couldn't get off work, I spent the day in the hospital waiting room by myself. It was a long day. My baby girl was having surgery. The surgery wasn't life-threatening, but for us it was still a traumatic event.

Looking at my phone, I was surprised to see a text message from Kevin.

*How is she doing?*

My cheap flip phone made it hard to text. There wasn't a little typing key pad, which made sending a text a chore. However, I was a happy, happy girl. We spent the entire day texting and getting to know each other. He worked diligently to keep me distracted and he did an amazing job.

Amanda's procedure went smoothly and it wasn't long until she was settled in a room for the night.

Thus began our online conversations and text messages which led to a conversation about our first meeting. I wasn't comfortable going on a date with someone I had never met, even if we were both in the same grade in high school. Mikyle's birthday was also coming up and I was trying to figure out how to celebrate his birthday on a tight budget.

"How to Train a Dragon" in 3D… with my mom, Mikyle and Ruby for Mikyle's birthday.

First date.

I was scared to death.

Scouring my closet for something decent to wear to see a movie in 3D on a blind date with your mother and son was rather difficult. What does one wear on such an occasion? While I was putting the finishing touches on my makeup, my phone dinged, alerting me to a new text message.

*Has anyone told you how big I am?* Kevin wrote.

I panicked. What in the world was he talking about? Instantly, the cynical victim advocate came out in me. What if he was really some creepy, 500 pound guy who stalked women on the internet and that wasn't even really his picture at all? It was too late to get out of it. I was taking my son … OMGOSH … I was taking my MOTHER.

*Ummm… no…?*

*I'm 6'5"!*

Huge sigh of relief, mingled with laughter. He was TALL! Not BIG. Not CREEPY. I am not opposed to BIG… however, I am only 5'5" so size, for a survivor, can be a super scary thing. Not to mention that I was rather over dramatic in my visualization of his actual being.

*"Oh … no worries … that doesn't scare me."* … *Much!*

The three of us made our way to our local movie theatre, a little early, I might add, to pick up our tickets and so I could appear calm, cool and collected. Mikyle scooted off to drool over all the arcade games while I kept a vigil at the front window, watching the parking lot.

It didn't take long before I saw him. I could see his head, above all of the vehicles, moving from the back of the lot toward the door. I could feel my heart pounding in my chest as he moved closer. Then I saw Ruby as, together, they made their way for the door. Hand in hand, they were walking, fearlessly, into our lives.

Awkward is such a weird word, but oh so fitting.

"Hi." We both looked at each other. Standing next to him in the crowded foyer, I realized my head stopped at his armpit. He was TALL. Craning my neck to see his face, my heart missed a beat when I looked into those eyes. I had spent weeks serendipitously looking at the sweetness in his eyes from his picture on Facebook. Now here he was, standing before me.

Kevin, the gentle giant, maintained his cool composure while I on the other hand, was sure the world could see that I was about to explode with nerves. I was sure it was written all across my forehead "FIRST DATE FREAK OUT" or something equally obnoxious.

Juggling tickets, drinks, popcorn and 3D glasses, we made our way to the theatre. Mikyle, always the blonde-haired, blue-eyed flirt, was out of his mind with excitement at watching a movie with a pretty girl. He was constantly in motion, everywhere we went. I never knew from moment to moment what kind of mischief he would find, adding to the frazzled state of my nerves. I was certainly going to need medication once this ordeal was over. Kevin and his pretty little counterpart may never want anything else to do with us ever.

We made our way to our seats and settled in. Everyone else had on their lovely and stylish 3D glasses but me. Kevin wore his proudly like the awesome dad that he is. I, on the other hand, wanted to pull off the "cute blonde bombshell" look. It only took me a few minutes to realize how dumb that was, and I settled back to watch the movie, glasses and all.

After the movie was over and we headed back to the lobby to say our goodbyes, I wasn't sure what Kevin was thinking. His face was an expressionless mask.

Out of the blue, Mikyle grabbed Ruby, who appeared rather annoyed by the whole "boy" thing, in a bear hug and planted a big kiss on her cheek. "Thank you for coming to my birthday." It was the sweetest thing I had ever seen. We all laughed and the date was over.

After awkward goodbyes were said and we headed back to our own vehicles.

I wasn't sure if I would ever hear from him again.

## Chapter 18

My phone rang after we got home from the movies. I was relieved to see it was him.

"I just want to say one thing."

"Okay…."

"I want you to give me a chance and let it be my game to lose. If this relationship doesn't work, it'll be my fault. Not yours."

Another layer began to crumble in the wall around my heart. There was no way he could know my insecurities. There was no way he could see into my heart. I was totally unprepared for the wave of intense, deep emotion that swept over my soul that night as a God-sent true love began to take root in the depths of my heart.

I had this list in my head of what I thought I was looking for in a mate right down to the spiritual traits my helpmate must possess. I thought I had it all figured out. I knew better than anyone what I needed. However, for all of my searching, for all of my failed relationships, I still failed to see that I was not in control of anything. For in the darkest hours of the night, as I lay awake in my bed dreaming of my future, there was still an eerie whisperer that planted seeds of thought into my spirit meant to draw me far away from the things that would bring me true happiness. Constantly doubting myself and my ability to have a good relationship, I kept looking for the points that would prove that *if it seems too good to be true, then it probably is.*

Kevin followed up the movie date by bringing Mikyle a Marshmallow gun he had made for his birthday. Of course, Ruby got one too, for it was the only way to have a marshmallow battle. It was a great day (except for the mini-marshmallows that covered the entire square footage of my home).

My brother, his wife and kids made their first journey to visit as a family the following week. Kevin just naturally fit with our crew. I marveled at our new found friendship as we sat around on my patio, barbequed on the grill and just visited with friends and family. It felt like we had known each other our entire lives. It felt comfortable and natural for us to be together.

We found ourselves talking for hours. Our evening hours were usually spent together, with the kids, either at the park or McDonald's playland. He would take Ruby home to stay with her grandmother while I put Mikyle to bed. Then he would come back to my house and we would sit in the quiet of the evening and share the stories of our lives with each other until neither one of us could stay awake. He would head home and the next day we would do it again.

"Let's make a deal. We will build our friendship for at least a year before we even think about getting serious or have serious discussions about our future." I agreed. A friend once told me that dating for an entire year gives you the chance to see how your families blend at every holiday and birthday. You also get to see the good days and the bad. We talked about every life scenario we could think of to see how we would handle things as a couple. The conversations were weird because it felt like we were made for each other.

Our mothers raised us in much the same way. And because their cooking styles were even the same, we both liked a lot of the same foods. It was amazing. It was almost too good to be true. He also shared with me details from his past. Mistakes he had made, regrets that he had about life, family and raising children. Because he put all of his cards on the table right from the start, I knew what I was getting out of the deal. I was in. Although we both made the deal to not get serious, it was serious from the start. We both knew it. There was no denying the bond that was already forming between us.

It seemed as if God was laying out all of the reasons for us to be together and the ways in which our relationship worked. Mikyle was obsessed with the movie "Cars" and he loved Lightning McQueen. Ruby loved princesses. Before our paths ever crossed, Mom found one of those balls with a handle that kids sit on and bounce, at a garage sale. It was purple. It had princesses on it. Mom bought it for Mikyle and insisted that it was "all right." No one would ever know he was playing with a girl's ball. Little did I know that another grandmother across town would also find the same type ball at a garage sale but her ball was red … with Lightning McQueen on it. As soon as the kids discovered this, they traded balls and all was right in the universe. It was one of those "God" moments.

We had two children each. One grown and one still at home: Zachary and Ruby were Kevin's and Mikyle and Amanda were mine. My kids were the opposite: my oldest was a girl and my youngest was a boy. The two oldest are eerily alike in their interests and tastes. The two youngest are vastly different, yet since Ruby is a tomboy, they got along fabulously.

"I don't want a relationship built on sex. It

was your heart that got my attention from the very beginning. Even though you are beautiful on the outside, I fell in love with your heart."

This was his constant refrain and he continued to show me what a gentleman he was. I wasn't quite sure how to handle a relationship built on friendship. Our first kiss happened over a month into our dating. He had already gone home for the night and I texted him to tease him about if he was ever going to kiss me goodnight.

He drove all the way back to my house to kiss me goodnight. I opened the front door to let him in and his nervousness was apparent. The wall around my heart melted a bit more. As he walked toward me, I could see he was shaking from head to toe. As he placed his hands on my arms to pull me closer, I could feel his hands trembling. He was ever so gentle as our lips touched for the first time. It was the sweetest, purest, kiss of my whole life.

Our favorite day was spent at Dinosaur Valley State Park. We hiked the trails, looked at dinosaur tracks and then sat on a bench and talked for hours. We held hands and felt something shift in our relationship.

Our Facebook friends watched our relationship blossom and grow.

*What an awesome weekend ... spent Saturday in Dinosaur Valley with a girl that makes me feel like a teenager, when I'm actually 3.25 teenagers ... came back to Oak Ridge, and had the most memorable sunset EVER ... started the day at church. (I think) I've found a home. Picked up baby girl and took her and Mikyle fishing at Uncle Bob's ... best of all, IT finally happened... 'IT' being, she sang to me ... most beautiful voice I've ever heard ... it made Ruby stop playing, and sit in my lap to listen ... unreal. Now, I'm defenseless ... putty ... just saying.*

I couldn't believe this relationship was really happening. I needed so desperately for it to be real. Mikyle also craved a dad so badly that it was just heartbreaking. He and Ruby bugged us constantly for us to get together so they could play. They had become great buddies. Ruby's heart was also crying out for stability. At four, it was a huge transition to go from living with both of her parents to living with her dad and not seeing her mom very often. Everything just made sense for us to be together.

There was, however, opposition to our relationship. People who knew the before-Christ Kevin were afraid that he wouldn't be good for me. The battle raged on inside of me. My heart grew more and more attached, but everyone else's opinions kept me wondering if it was the right decision. Also, he had been married for twenty years. I didn't want to be his rebound relationship. I didn't want to be his second choice. I knew I deserved better than that. In my own marriage, I was second best to all of the women my ex cheated with. I wanted, needed, to be first choice.

Love, faith, trust and insecurities all battled within my heart. I never knew from day to day which one would win. It didn't take much for my insecurities and lack of trust to rise to the surface. Not answering the phone or text quickly enough was enough to send me into a panic. Convinced he was going to leave me like everyone else, I promised myself that he wouldn't get the chance.

I couldn't risk having my heart broken again but I couldn't face him to tell him. So, I resorted back to how our relationship originally began. Text.

*I'm sorry, but I can't do this.* I typed out the words and before I could change my mind, I hit the send button.

The phone rang.

"I don't even deserve a phone call?"

"I'm sorry."

We talked for a little while and I wanted to scream and cry. I didn't want to end it, but the pressure kept coming from every direction and I didn't know what else to do. He agreed to let me go. I wanted him to fight for our relationship.

He unfriended me on Facebook, but we still talked on the phone and text as friends. I couldn't resist that pull between us, the cord that would not be broken. I couldn't help it. I didn't want it to be over.

He baited the line and set the hook….

"I'm going to start seeing other people. I just wanted to let you know."

I stared at the phone like a monster had appeared on the other end.

"What do you mean, you're going to see other people?"

"Well ... if you're sure we can't be together, then there's no sense in my waiting around for you to change your mind."

I swallowed it, hook, line and sinker. Panic started to swell up in my heart. I didn't want to lose him. I just wanted all of the negative voices to be quiet and leave us alone.

I surrendered. Life continued and we grew closer and closer.

A few months later, another bout of indecision struck me and I couldn't make up my mind if I should go forward in the relationship. Kevin had never done a single thing wrong. We never had a single argument. He never got angry or upset with me, but I couldn't shake the feelings. Trusting anyone was hard. I didn't want to get hurt. I couldn't overcome it. Just when I thought I had, doubts and questions would come barreling back to hit me right between the eyes again. I was scared.

Kevin got up off the couch and headed for the door. "You know, I have done everything I'm supposed to do. I've never wavered, but there comes a time when I have to stop and think about what's best for me and my kids, too. I need a few days to think about things."

It was dusk when he walked out that door. He was just a shadow as he stepped away from the porch light. My heart ached as I watched him walk out the door. I was used to all of the familiar ugly voices from my past that whispered in my ear. However, this night it was different. The whisper in my spirit was soft and gentle. I felt a peace and comfort settle over my spirit that the message was pure and true ... "There goes your future."

The words hit me like a ton of bricks. He was a good man. He was an amazing father. He had a good heart. He had laid out every mistake, every dream and every hurt before me like a sacrifice to prove himself worthy of my love. I had been so caught up in my own issues that I had missed the essence of what an amazing man I was allowing to walk out of my life. I couldn't handle the thought that I had lost him forever.

The time spent apart hurt, a gut wrenching, life-is-over kind of hurt. We were both miserable. I surrendered. I had no choice. Good or bad, mistake or not, I would never know for sure if I didn't give it my all. It was time to stop wandering in my life's desert of darkness and to finally walk into a future full of promise.

We talked through all of my worries and doubts. The future started to shine brightly before me. There was still so much to overcome, but I knew that together we could make it through anything.

*Poll time, peeps: Do you believe in "love at first sight?' Possible? Impossible? Proof."* Kevin also tried to make sense of what was happening in our lives. We both had pasts, hurts, children with hurts and uncertain futures. We knew just two things for sure: 1. We wanted God in the middle of whatever was happening and, 2. We couldn't resist the connection between us.

That Christmas, Amanda shared her heart with me. She was no longer my little girl. Somewhere along the way she became this beautiful young woman with a career and a bright future. She was a college graduate working as a designer. My heart swelled with pride. We both had our scars. The battle for survival had been fierce, but somehow we both made it through. My biggest regret was the damage I had done to my precious baby girl. It was the hardest thing to forgive, keeping her so long in that house.

"Mom, I just want to let you know, that if you

and Kevin get to the point where you are serious, I give you my blessing."

All the love in my heart for this child bubbled over and she gave me her classic "Amanda" look and said, "Don't mess it up. I like this one."

I burst out laughing.

God was healing.

He was restoring and life was good.

Sitting in my office, a few months later, my phone signaled a text message.

*Will you do me the honor of becoming my wife?*

I stared at the words on my phone unsure if he was serious or not. I was still not always sure when he, always the prankster, was being serious, but I chose to receive it as a serious proposal. That way he couldn't back out.

## Chapter 19

As surely as the stars shine in the night sky, I know that God is gracious in his love for me. He knows the intimate secrets of my heart and my most treasured desires as well. My biological father accepted my friend request on Father's Day in 2010, and when I posted about our upcoming wedding I never expected the call that I received.

"Hey kiddo, I was wondering if you would mind if I came to Texas to attend your wedding."

He had no way of knowing my childhood dream of being Daddy's little girl. He had no idea that I had searched for him my entire life. I had always wondered why I wasn't good enough, or why he didn't love me enough to be in my life. I, like every other little girl from the beginning of time, wanted my daddy to walk me down the aisle.

It felt as if the heavens had opened and God Himself was handing me this huge and precious gift… my dad. Trying to maintain my composure, I hoped I could hold it together to respond.

"I would LOVE to have you come to my wedding. I would love for you to walk me down the aisle."

"Wow. I wasn't expecting that you would even consider me walking you down the aisle."

Friends and family all came together to help us plan our celebration.

My dad arrived from Michigan, and it felt like we had all known him and been around him our whole lives. The fear of awkward moments quickly disappeared as our hearts connected and we were reminded over and over that we were truly blood-related.

The uncomfortably hot July weather was typical for Texas, but neither the heat nor the work setting up the wedding could damper our spirits. Each moment that drew us closer to that moment lent its hand at healing the breach in my spirit.

I was learning that the Biblical meaning of submission and a batterer's view of submission are two different things. It's easy to 'submit' to a man who truly resembles Christ. For a man to love a wife as Christ loves the church is an amazing gift of surrender and sacrifice, for Christ laid down His life for His bride. A husband with this nature puts the needs, insecurities and doubts included, of his wife above his own needs and tenderly seeks out ways to satisfy his bride's heart. I have learned that "submission" does not mean servant or slave. Submission means respect and consideration, and of that Kevin is well deserving.

The festivities of the day were overwhelming for Mikyle, but he was excited to be getting a dad. There was no amount of medication that could calm his ADHD that day. As we finished the final details for the day, Mikyle and his newfound grandpa went back to the hotel to swim in the pool and relax for a while. It was a great diversion. The emotions of the day got the best of my seven year old.

Amanda made a beautiful bridesmaid in her long, pink, floral dress. Ruby played the role of our adorable flower girl with a wreath of red roses crowning her head of brown curls. Zachary, standing nearly as tall as his daddy, represented his father well as best man.

Proudly, I walked down the aisle on the arm of my earthly father. With my heart full to overflowing, I could barely contain my joy. I looked at the decorated altar, in Kevin's childhood church and I saw our children and the man that God had chosen for my husband

and my heart was filled with peace. For the first time in my life I felt the weight of the past lift and with it went the old battered sign I had worn upon my heart called "unworthy." On this day, it was replaced with a new sign: BELOVED.

For all of the years that were lost in the abyss of abuse and the pain that had crushed my spirit to a smoldering pile of ashes, God had raised up something beautiful from the dust. He had taken the hurts of two broken families and forged them together in love with a cord so strong that the puppet master could not touch it.

Our vows were sealed and represented with a jar of sand, three colors in all. Unity of lives, it represented, husband, wife, and Holy Spirit bound together with children to create one. We call it family.

Our sweet brother in Christ and pastor friend issued the beloved command, "You may kiss your bride." Ever so sweetly, our lips touched and the final cord from the past was broken. A new, a three-strand cord, bound our hearts and lives together. Our promise to each other was captured in that moment, a pinky swear: divorce would never be an option and would never be placed on the table. Till death do us part.

With that sacred stage set, the puppet master and his apprentices slithered away into the night. His wiles and his plans were no match for true love. The God and creator of the universe had a much greater plan for our lives. The stage of our future is set, the adventures are yet to be seen. I'm grateful that through love's grace, I learned that only *Hope Reigns*.

## *Prologue*

The "Puppet Master" woven throughout this book is ultimately power and control. Many people mistakenly believe domestic violence is a mental illness or an anger management issue. It is not. It is the learned behavior of one person to exert power and control over another human being. Some might also assume that the "Puppet Master" is the dark presence of evil, or Satan, if you will. You decide!

Many survivors go on to live their lives after an abusive relationship is over settling and merely getting by. Many think they have totally healed and overcome the trauma. Others do not realize the many ways in which those old learned behaviors are still impacting their lives. There is amazing liberty in being able to recognize these cords of control and breaking them once and for all!

One by one God has exposed those cords of control in my own life. I have learned ways to deal with the triggers, flashbacks, and other behaviors that remind me that I once was a victim. I, not only deal with them, I overcome them! It is not His will or plan that anyone should remain bound by the negative impact of their past trauma. Healing and moving forward is possible!

My heart's desire for this book was to share my journey, my struggles and my heart. I pray that those who don't understand domestic violence may understand it better because of my journey. I also hope that it will give survivors the courage to remove their masks and be real and honest about their struggles and pain. The journey to recovery is not easy. I wish it was.

My hope is that everyone will find something of themselves in my story whether it be abuse, abandonment, divorce, new career, single parenting, etc. We all have wounds and hurts. We all wear masks. I hope you can relate.

There are many views and definition of forgiveness. We all have own way of processing hurts and coming to terms with our own beliefs regarding this topic. Our personal belief system on this subject will directly impact the level to which we can be healed and set free from wounds caused by others. It can also directly impact the degree to which we remain bound in our hurts. We all forgive in our own time, even when we feel pressured by others to forgive quickly. It isn't always that easy when the wounds are deep and raw. I struggled with the meaning of forgiveness for a long time until I realized that forgiveness doesn't mean reconciliation of a relationship. It doesn't mean that you have to put yourself back into an unhealthy environment.

Forgiveness is meant more for the one who was hurt than the one who did the hurting. I was able to forgive my ex fairly easily for the things he did to me. It was harder to forgive him for the pain he caused our daughter. I struggled for a long time with that. The hardest of all was to forgive myself. Ultimately, forgiveness is a deliberate choice we make. It is liberating and it brings healing.

A friend once told me that you will know when you have forgiven someone when you begin to see that person as a victim. There is much wisdom and truth in that statement. Whenever I picture my ex in my mind, I see a little boy, with big brown eyes and long curly eyelashes (the male version of my daughter) and I see his hurt. We were both victims. Our families were victims. There were no winners. We all lost.

I did not write this book to cause my ex-husband or his family pain. That is not my desire. I did not write this book to say that I am all good and he is all bad. I made my share of mistakes every step of the way. I own my part of the failure of our marriage but I don't own the abuse. I was not responsible for another person's decision to batter. I wrote this book to share the journey so others can understand the darkness that comes from violence. I also wanted to share with the world my love story with my Heavenly Father and the gift of love from the husband of my dreams.

Amanda has blossomed into an amazing young woman. I am so proud to call her my daughter. She graduated college at nineteen and was hired directly after graduation as a lead designer for a cheer company. After a few years, her company was sold to a larger cheer company who hired her as a couture designer. She is currently working as a freelance designer and is starting her own photography business. In addition to that, she is also using her love of photography to make survivors (of cancer, abuse, and adversities of life) beautiful through her own non-profit organization.

She married her fiancé three months after I married Kevin. My dad and step-mom were there for her wedding as well. We are so blessed. God has done amazing things in her life. He has restored so much in our lives.

I can't imagine any blended family being able to come together, in love, any better than what God orchestrated in ours. We don't use the word "step" in our home. We are family. I'm grateful I didn't give up all those years ago. Even though leaving was the hardest thing I have ever done in my life, it was the first step toward an amazing future.

I hope my story has inspired, educated and given you hope as well!

## About The Author

Mary Farmer is a dynamic motivational speaker and Bible teacher who travels the country sharing her message of hope. She is also a worship leader and Christian recording artist. Her unique flare for combining music into her presentations keeps her audience on the edge of their seats as she shares her story of triumph. She also provides valuable trainings, workshops and seminars on domestic violence, its effects and how to work with victims. Mary's heart is to see survivor's overcome the long lasting effects of abuse, to heal and triumph over their pasts.

Her story has been featured in major publications, such as: *Good Housekeeping* Magazine in 2011 and *Marie Claire* Australia in 2012.

Mary has founded two non-profits and worked as the Executive Director and victim advocate for eight years at the crisis center she founded. She is also a certified Restorative Faith Based Counselor and Certified Life Coach. She currently coaches new ministry non-profits in addition to her speaking schedule.

Mary and her husband have a blended family with four children, two dogs and a cat. They enjoy a country lifestyle in East Texas. Their family ministry provides mentoring and support for other ministries and new non-profits.

If you are in danger and need help, please, call the National Domestic Violence Hotline for assistance:

*1-800-799-7233*

For more information about domestic violence and the Farmer Family's Ministry:
www.farmerfamilyministries.org

To book Mary to speak or sing:
Email: maryfarmerfm@gmail.com

www.maryfarmer.com

You can also listen to her weekly broadcast on Blogtalkradio:

*Hope Reigns with Mary Farmer*

www.ingramcontent.com/pod-product-compliance
Lightning Source LLC
Chambersburg PA
CBHW031145020426
42333CB00013B/522